STRUCTURAL DETAILS FOR CONCRETE CONSTRUCTION

D1478117

Companion Volumes

Newman . Structural Details for Masonry Construction
Newman . Structural Details for Steel Construction
Newman . Structural Details for Wood Construction

STRUCTURAL DETAILS FOR CONCRETE CONSTRUCTION

Morton Newman, P.E.

PROJECT EDITOR: Jeremy Robinson

McGRAW-HILL BOOK COMPANY

New York   St. Louis   San Francisco   Auckland
Bogotá   Hamburg   London   Madrid   Mexico
Milan   Montreal   New Delhi   Panama
Paris   São Paulo   Singapore
Sydney   Tokyo   Toronto

3-91

16277990

Library of Congress Cataloging-in-Publication Data

Newman, Morton.
    Structural details for concrete construction.

    "The material in this volume has been published pre-
viously in Standard structural details for building
construction"—T.p. verso.
    Includes index.
    1. Concrete construction. 2. Building—Details—Drawing.
I. Newman, Morton. Standard structural details for
building construction. II. Title.
TA681.5.N49   1988   690'.5   87-17075
ISBN 0-07-046360-3 (pbk.)

1234567890   KGP/KGP   893210987

ISBN 0-07-046360-3

Printed and bound by Arcata Graphics/Kingsport

To my mother

Contents

About This Book

Since publication in 1968, over 30,000 copies of the hardcover edition of Morton Newman's STANDARD STRUCTURAL DETAILS FOR BUILDING CONSTRUCTION have been sold to architects, engineers, drafters, and others concerned with the design of building structure and the communication of that design to those responsible for accomplishing it in construction.

Now the publishers have made it possible for persons interested in one particular type of structure—wood, concrete, masonry, or steel—to purchase just the section or sections of *Standard Structural Detals* which they need. The hardcover book has been split up into four separate low-cost softcover editions:

Structural Details for Wood Construction
Structural Details for Concrete Construction
Structural Details for Masonry Construction
Structural Details for Steel Construction

In this book, the designer will find a host of proven designs in timetested details for continuous footings; grade beams; pit walls; basement walls; reinforcement splices and bends; retaining walls; beam sections; concrete joists; caissons; spread footings; column sections; and splices, slabs, steps, and precast walls.

Introductory material has been revised to reflect code changes since the original edition, and each page of details appears on the right, while facing pages incorporate a preprinted grid for drawings, notes, and ideas the reader may wish to preserve.

Preface

The purpose of this series of books is to provide a graphic means of communication between architects, engineers, contractors, and students who are engaged in the design and construction of buildings. The four basic structural materials that are employed in building construction are wood, concrete, masonry, and steel. In the application of these materials many standard details and methods of construction have been developed. For several years the author found it quite useful to collect and index standard structural details for the preparation of structural drawings of buildings. The use of structural graphic standards reduced the cost of production of structural drawings and also helped to facilitate the communication of information between all of the personnel who were involved in the design and construction of a building. No claim is made for the originality of the details in these books as they are standard methods of construction and they are extensively used throughout the construction industry.

These books consist of a series of drawings of standard structural details that are most frequently employed in building construction. The details are presented individually and in their most basic and general form. A brief description is given for each detail pertaining to the material used, the type of condition shown, and its method of construction. In no instance should a book be considered or used as a substitute for the engineer or as a shortcut method of engineering. It is the function of the engineer to verify the use of any detail and to determine the sizes, dimensions, and all other pertinent information that will be essential to its use in a particular building design. The details are separated and arranged into four books with respect to the type of construction materials used: wood, concrete, masonry, or steel. In some instances two types of construction materials are used in the same detail. The author endeavored to place each detail in the related book and in the sequence of its use in building construction so that it could be readily located. Also, the index for this book has been set up so that any particular detail that may be sought can be easily located.

The engineering information presented in these books is in accordance with the basic requirements of The American Institute of Steel Construction, The American Concrete Institute, The International Conference of Building Officials Uniform Building Code, "The West Coast Lumbermen's Douglas Fir Use Book," and The Concrete Masonry Association of California. Standard details and construction methods evolve from the structural design requirements. Many excellent books on structural design and analysis are available to the practicing engineer and student; there is also a great need for applied practical information related to structural drafting and the use of construction materials. Expanding technology in the fields of building engineering and construction has created a situation which demands that the structural drawings be more complete and therefore more complex.

The purpose of structural drawings is to communicate the engineer's design requirements to the various contractors and material fabricators.

To achieve total communication, the structural drawings should be clear and complete, the general presentation of information should be in a logical sequence, all sections and details should be shown and clearly referenced, and any field conditions should be considered on the drawings. A good set of structural drawings will ensure that the building is constructed in accordance with the engineering design requirements and that construction delays and unnecessary additional costs are avoided.

The engineer's work is the prime factor in the successful design and construction of a building; however, in the final event, his or her work is directly dependent upon the intelligence and integrity of the workers on the construction job, particularly at the supervisory level. Poor fieldwork in terms of accuracy and material quality control will negate a great deal of engineering effort. Building construction requires a high degree of teamwork between the engineers and the contractors. Each party should have a working knowledge of the other's functions and responsibilities. The author hopes that these books will serve as communication tools that will improve the quality of engineering and construction. Also, engineering and architectural students can use this book as a source of information to familiarize themselves with the methods and materials of construction. As students use the information presented in these books, they will increase their ability to translate structural engineering calculations into practical applications.

I would like to acknowledge the very able assistance of Bruce L. Ward, who drew the details shown on the following pages and assisted in assembling the information into book form. Also, I would like to thank Jack Clark for his advice and encouragement, and acknowledge the assistance of Bogdan Todorovic in the early stages of these books.

Morton Newman
Civil Engineer

Abbreviations

Adjustable	Adjust.	Existing	Exist.
Alternate	Alt.	Expand	Exp.
American Concrete Institute	A.C.I.	Expose	Expo.
American Institute of	A.I.S.C.	Exterior	Ext.
Steel Construction			
American Society of	A.S.T.M.	Fillet	Fill.
Testing and Materials		Finish	Fin.
Architect	Arch.	Floor	Flr.
Area	A.	Foot	Ft.
		Footing	Ftg.
Beam	Bm.	Foundation	Fdn.
Block	Blk.	Framing	Frmg.
Blocking	Blkg.		
Bottom	Bott.	Gauge	Ga.
Building	Bldg.	Glued Laminated	Gl. Lam.
		Grade	Gr.
Calculations	Calcs.	Grout	Grt.
Ceiling	Ceil.	Gypsum	Gyp.
Cement	Cem.		
Center Line	C.L.	Hanger	Hngr.
Channel Stud	C.S.	Height	Ht.
Civil Engineer	C.E.	Hook	Hk.
Clear	Clr.	Horizontal	Horiz.
Column	Col.		
Concrete	Conc.		
Connection	Conn.	Inch	In.
Construction	Constr.	Inclusive	Incl.
Continuous	Cont.	Inside Diameter	I.D.
Cubic	Cu.	Interior	Int.
Deflection	Defl.	Joint	Jnt.
Depression	Depr.	Joist	Jst.
Detail	Det.		
Diagonal	Diag.	Lag Screw	L.S.
Diameter	Dia.	Laminated	Lam.
Dimension	Dim.	Lateral	Lat.
Discontinuous	Disc.	Light Weight	Lt. Wt.
Double	Dbl.		
Drawing	Drwg.	Machine	Mach.
		Masonry	Mas.
Each	Ea.	Maximum	Max.
Elevation	El. or Elev.	Membrane	Memb.
Engineer	Engr.	Metal	Met. or Mtl.
Equal	Eq.	Minimum	Min.
Equipment	Equip.	Moment of Inertia	I

Nails	d (penny)	Sheathing	Shtg.
Natural	Nat.	Sheet	Sht.
Number	No. or #	Spacing	Spcg.
		Specification	Spec.
On Center	O.C.	Spiral	Sp.
Opening	Opng.	Stagger	Stgr.
Opposite	Opp.	Standard	Std.
Outside Diameter	O.D.	Steel	Stl.
		Steel Joist	S.J.
Panels	Pnls.	Stiffener	Stiff.
Partition	Part.	Stirrup	Stirr.
Penetration	Pen.	Structural	Struct.
Plaster	Plas.	Structural Steel Tube	S.S.T.
Plate	Pl.	Square	Sq.
Plywood	Plywd.	Symmetrical	Sym.
Pounds per Cubic Foot	P.C.F.		
Pounds per Square Foot	P.S.F.	Thick	Thk.
Pounds per Square Inch	P.S.I.	Through	Thru.
Pressure	Press.	Tread	Tr.
Radius	R.	Ultimate	Ult.
Rafter	Rftr.	Ultimate Stress Design	U.S.D.
Rectangular	Rect.	Uniform Building Code	U.B.C.
Reinforcing	Reinf.	Utility	Util
Required	Reqd.		
Riser	R.	Vertical	Vert.
Roof	Rf.	Volume	Vol.
Room	Rm.		
Round	φ	Waterproof	W.P.
		Weight	Wt.
Schedule	Sched.	Welded Wire Fabric	W.W.F.
Section	Sect.	Wide Flange	W.F.
Section Modulus	S.	With	W/
Seismic	Seis.	Working Stress Design	W.S.D.

INTRODUCTION

The details shown in this volume pertain to reinforced concrete construction. Since each of the following drawings is presented in its most general form, many of the dimensions and structural sizes are omitted. It is required that these dimensions and sizes be determined by engineering design calculation for each specific condition of use of the detail.

The details are arranged in the following general categories: continuous footings for walls, grade beams, pit walls, basement walls, wall openings, retaining walls, beam sections, poured-in-place belled caissons, spread footings, pile caps, column sections, slab sections, wall pilasters, and precast wall sections. Several of the details presented in this volume are composed of concrete and other construction materials such as wood, masonry, and steel. These details are included in this particular volume because their basic application in building relates to reinforced concrete construction.

The type and the strength of the concrete required for the construction of the details in this chapter are not specified. The requirements for structural concrete of a building depend upon the concrete durability, watertightness, and resistance to deterioration; the economics of the construction; and the strength of the concrete that will be needed to resist the dead and live loads. Structural concrete strength is determined by its capacity to resist compression and is expressed as a unit compressive stress in terms of pounds per square inch. The unit compressive stress that is used to specify the strength of a concrete mixture 28 days after it is placed or molded for test samples is denoted as f'_c. The values of f'_c for the various water and cement mixtures of concrete are verified by testing the compression resistance of a certain number of standard size specimen samples. The American Society for Testing and Materials specifies definite and rigid requirements for the testing procedures of concrete specimen. The specimen samples are taken from fresh concrete batches and molded into cylinders 6″ in diameter and 12″ high or are taken from cores of existing concrete. These test cylinders are subjected to loads to determine their ultimate compressive strength at 7 days and at 28 days after the sample is molded and cured. The results of the tests of a number of specimen of a particular concrete mixture can give a comparatively wide range of values for the compressive strength. In order to obtain a valid value of the f'_c, it is necessary to test several specimen samples of a mixture and correlate the results mathematically. The statistical standard deviation and the coefficient of variation are used to indicate the degree of quality control of the concrete mixture. The standard deviation is obtained by subtracting the square root of the average of the squares of all the test result values from the common average value. The coefficient of variation is a percentage determined by dividing the standard deviation by the mean value of the test results. Proper quality control of concrete mixtures should produce concrete with an average compressive strength of 15% greater than the f'_c for working stress designs and 25% greater for ultimate stress designs. The design, testing, sampling, and evaluating of concrete mixtures are performed by a responsible laboratory using definite standards of procedure.

Structural concrete is generally specified by the water-cement ratio of the mixture, the value of f'_c, and the weight or the volume proportions of the mixture. Concrete is composed of a mixture of cement, water, coarse aggregate, fine aggregate, and, in certain cases, chemical admixtures. The type and quality of cement used in commercial structural concrete is Type I portland cement, which is produced in accordance with rigid A.S.T.M. standards. Other types of commercial cements are available; however, Type I cement is most commonly used in building construction. Fine aggregate and coarse aggregate are two different materials in the concrete mixture; however, both are used as chemically inert fillers to increase the volume of the mixture. Coarse aggregates consist of particles of crushed rock greater than $\frac{1}{4}''$ but usually not larger than $1\frac{1}{2}''$. Fine aggregates consist of graded natural sand and particles of crushed rock less than $\frac{1}{4}''$. Various types of aggregate can be employed in concrete to achieve a specific quality that may be required as a condition of the use of the concrete; for example, concrete used for fireproofing or thermal insulation requires a lightweight mixture. Many commercial chemical admixtures are also available for use in structural concrete. These admixtures are used to produce a specific quality in the finished concrete such as watertightness, hard exterior surfaces, color, and high early strength immediately after the concrete is placed.

The water-cement ratio of a concrete mixture is the primary factor in determining the compressive strength of the hardened concrete. The water and cement combine chemically to create a physical paste which adheres to and binds the aggregates. The result of this chemical and physical phenomenon is a concrete mixture that will act as a monolithic material after it hardens. The water-cement ratio is usually specified as the number of gallons of water per sack of cement. This ratio can also be expressed in terms of weight or in the number of cubic feet of water and the number of cubic feet of cement. One cubic foot of water equals 7.48 gal.; one standard sack of cement equals 1 cu. ft. These values are given to demonstrate arithmetically that a water-cement ratio of 7.5 gal. of water per sack of cement will contain approximately 1 cu. ft. of water per cubic foot of cement. The compressive strength of concrete is inversely proportional to the water-cement ratio; that is, as the water-cement ratio increases, the f'_c value decreases. The f'_c values of structural concrete range between 2000 and 5000 psi and are usually designated in 500 psi increments, except for $f'_c = 3750$ psi.

Efficient methods for the proper placing of concrete depend upon the plasticity or workability of the wet mixture. The degree of plasticity of wet concrete is determined by a slump test. This test is performed by measuring the subsidence or vertical displacement of a sample of the wet concrete mixture. The sample is formed in a metal truncated cone 12″ high with top and bottom diameters equal to 4″ and 8″, respectively. The results of the test are given as the number of inches of vertical displacement that is measured immediately after the cone form is removed. The amount of slump should vary between 2″ and 6″. The required degree of plasticity depends on the clearance between reinforcing bars, the size of the coarse aggregate, the method of delivering the concrete to the forms, and the intricacy of the formwork. The A.C.I. Building Code recommends a maximum slump of 4″ and a minimum slump of 1″ with respect to the various structural elements of the building.

The minimum slump value should be maintained for construction of concrete ramps, sloping walls, and slabs. When the slump is high, the wet concrete mixture will be loose and thus permit the coarse aggregates to separate from the cement paste; when the slump is low, the wet concrete mixture may be stiff and will create internal void spaces in the hardened concrete. Very often the wet concrete must be mechanically vibrated or rodded as it is placed to prevent the formation of internal voids and to ensure that the reinforcing bars are completely surrounded by concrete. Mechanical vibrating should be performed with care so that the designed positions of the reinforcing bars will not be altered. The design of reinforced concrete is based on the condition that the concrete material is homogeneous and well consolidated when it is placed; if this condition is met, the concrete will react as a monolithic material when it hardens. A positive physical bond must exist between the reinforcement and the concrete. Internal voids that are caused by poor consolidation will seriously reduce the structural bonding of the two different materials. Also, reinforcement surfaces should be free of excessive rust and mill scale, paint, soil, or other substances that will reduce the bond capacity. To ensure good consolidation, concrete should be placed in continuous layers of uniform depth; it should not be dropped into place from a height greater than 5.0 ′ and it should not be chuted into place at a steep angle for long distances. Concrete mixes that are composed of small size aggregates are often used when the clearance dimensions between the reinforcing bars and between the forms are small. As the concrete is being placed, it should be continuously moved away from the sides of the forms to allow the smaller size aggregates to settle near the exposed surfaces and thus give the structure a smooth finish and eliminate surface voids.

After concrete is placed, it must be cured to obtain a uniform hardness. The curing process consists of creating an external and internal condition of temperature and moisture that will be favorable to the uniform hardening of concrete. The time rate of hardening is not constant; it proceeds quite rapidly immediately after the concrete is placed, and it will attain approximately 70% of its f'_c value within the first seven days. The concrete will continue to harden at a progressively slower rate

for a long period of time; however, it should attain at least the f'_c value within 28 days after it is in place. Cold weather, that is, temperatures less than 40°F, will retard the water and cement chemical reaction required to produce the cement paste in the mixture. Hot weather, that is, temperatures greater than 90°F, will cause the exposed surface moisture to evaporate, which will result in uneven hardening and surface cracks. The method and length of time required to cure a particular concrete construction should be determined with regard to the temperature and moisture conditions at the job site at the time the concrete is placed. The concrete should be kept moist for at least one day immediately after it is placed, and it should be prevented from rapid drying for seven days. High-early-strength concrete mixtures require only a three day curing period.

The formwork for a concrete structure is constructed to reflect the architectural- and engineering-designed configuration. Although concrete forms are generally designed and constructed by the contractor, the resident engineer or building inspector should verify that the forms satisfy two main conditions: (1) that the form structure is safe and (2) that the forms meet the architectural and engineering design requirements as they are shown on the working drawings. Since the formwork is often used as a working deck during construction, it should be designed and constructed to resist vertical and lateral forces. Many form failures are the result of improper or insufficient lateral bracing that was required to plumb the structure and to resist the lateral forces caused during construction. The contractor must provide sufficient vertical support shores of the form structure to prevent excessive deflections or the overstressing of any form members. The sides of beams, columns, and walls should be braced against the hydrostatic pressure exerted by the wet concrete mixture. These side forms may be removed as soon as the concrete attains its initial hardness; however, the vertical supporting members should not be removed until the concrete attains a strength capable of supporting the dead load of the structure and any construction live loads that may occur. The contact surfaces of the forms are coated with a heavy oil to prevent the concrete from adhering to the forms and to permit the forms to be removed without damaging the exposed concrete surfaces. Also, the sharp corners of rectangular columns, walls, and beams are formed with a 45° chamfer strip to eliminate the possibility of spalling the concrete when the forms are removed. Damaged concrete surfaces, surface voids, and form tie holes are patched with a patching mortar that is composed of the same proportions of sand and cement as the poured concrete. The surface finish of poured concrete depends on the degree of exposure of the members and the architectural quality of the building. The A.C.I. Standard 301-84 defines the various methods and criteria for concrete surface finishes.

Structural reinforced concrete members are used to resist external loads by reacting by bending, by compression, or by a combination of both bending and compression. The ability of plain concrete to resist tensile stress is quite low and undependable. In the analysis and design of reinforced concrete it is assumed that the concrete material offers no resistance to tensile stress and that the tension is resisted only by the reinforcing steel. Reinforcing steel is also used to resist compression in a member acting in flexure or compression when the unit compression exceeds the permissible compressive stress of the concrete.

The structural analysis is mathematically performed by the "transformed section method." This method is based on the assumptions that (1) the concrete resists compression, (2) the reinforcing steel resists tension and compression, (3) the concrete cannot resist tension, (4) the reinforcing steel and the concrete are bonded together and therefore react together, (5) the reinforcing steel and the concrete are individually elastic. When a reinforced concrete member deflects or deforms from an externally applied load, the unit stress in the reinforcing steel is directly proportional to the unit stress in the concrete. The proportional relationship between the two materials is denoted as n. The value n of a concrete mixture is defined as the ratio of the modulus of elasticity of the reinforcing steel E_s and the modulus of elasticity of the concrete E_c, or $n = 30,000/f'_c$. It can be seen in the last equation that n is inversely proportional to the value of f'_c. The values of n vary from 15.0 for $f'_c = 2000$ psi for n = 6.0 for $f'_c = 5000$ psi. The reinforcing steel area of a concrete beam or column can be converted or transformed into an equivalent cross section of concrete by multiplying the cross-sectional area of the reinforcement, A_s by the value of n. After the reinforced concrete is transformed into an analogous homogeneous concrete member, it can be structurally analyzed by the use of the basic rules of mechanics and equilibrium.

The working stress design (W.S.D.) method, as applied to reinforced concrete members, is performed by using maximum allowable working stresses of the materials, the actual dead load, and a specified live load. The various building codes and design criteria specify the maximum allowable design stress for concrete and reinforcing steel. These stresses are determined by dividing the yield point stress of the material by a factor of safety. Reinforced concrete structures designed by the working stress design method do not utilize the full stress capacity of the materials because the factor of safety is applied generally both to the working stresses of each material and to the loads.

Another method of reinforced concrete stuctural design is called the ultimate strength design (U.S.D.) method. This method is based upon designing the members to the yield point stress of the materials and by individually increasing the dead load and the live load by a particular load factor instead of by a single general safety factor. The ultimate strength design method is currently being adopted by many building codes and design criteria since it can effect a significant economy in the use of concrete and reinforcing steel and also create a structure that will more realistically react to the design loading.

Table 1 shows the various reinforcing steel strength values and their respective A.S.T.M. specification titles and numbers.

Reinforcing steel bars are manufactured in standard sizes which are designated by a number. Each designation number represents the number of eighths of an inch of the nominal diameter of a deformed reinforcing bar, for example, #5 or #6. Plain reinforcing

Table 1. Concrete Reinforcing Steel for A S T M Specifications

Minimum yield-point strength, psi	Grade of steel	A S T M specification title	A S T M Spec. No.
40,000	Intermediate	Specifications for Billet-steel Bars for Concrete Reinforcement	A 615
	Intermediate	Specifications for Axle-steel Bars for Concrete Reinforcement	A 617
	Intermediate	Specifications for Special Large Size Deformed Billet-steel Bars for Concrete Reinforcement	A 408
50,000	Hard	Specifications for Billet-steel Bars for Concrete Reinforcement	A 615
	Regular	Specifications for Rail-steel Bars for Concrete Reinforcement	A 616
	Hard	Specifications for Axle-steel Bars for Concrete Reinforcement	A 617
	Hard	Specifications for Special Large Size Deformed Billet-steel Bars for Concrete Reinforcement	A 408
60,000		Specifications for Low-Alloy Steel Deformed Bars for Concrete Reinforcement	A 706
70,000		Specifications for Cold-drawn Steel Wire for Concrete Reinforcement	A 82
150,000		Uncoated High-Strength Steel Bars for Prestressing Concrete	A 722
Bars and rod mats		Specifications for Fabricated Steel Bar or Rod Mats for Concrete Reinforcement	A 184
Welded wire fabric		Specifications for Welded Steel Wire Fabric for Concrete Reinforcement	A 185

bars, that is, bars that are not deformed, are designated as the diameter in inches, for example, $\frac{1}{2}''$ or $\frac{5}{8}''$. Reinforcing bars that are $\frac{1}{4}''$ in diameter are never deformed and are always designated as #2 bars. Reinforcing bars that are manufactured with a raised surface pattern are referred to as deformed bars. These surface projections serve to increase the contact area between the concrete and the reinforcing steel, and they also provide a mechanical device to increase the bar bond capacity. Welded wire fabric consists of cold-drawn wire arranged in a rectangular pattern and welded at the points of intersection. The size and the spacing of the wire can be varied in either direction. The welded wire fabric shown on the following drawings is $6 \times 6 - 10/10$; the 6×6 indicates that the wires are 6″ o.c. in each direction, and the 10/10 indicates that the wires are 10 gauge in each direction. Cold-drawn wire or plain reinforcing rod that is used for round column spiral reinforcement is designated as the rod diameter in inches. Table 2 shows the reinforcing bar designation numbers and their dimensions.

Reinforcing bars should be accurately placed to ensure that the completed construction will reflect the engineer's design. Small inaccuracies may appreciably increase the stress in a member and thus cause serious surface cracks; therefore the engineer must rely a great deal on the intelligence and the integrity of the workers who are constructing the designs. Shop drawings prepared from the information given on the engineer's working drawings will help to coordinate the fieldwork with the structural design. The engineer responsible for the structural design should check the shop drawings for dimensions, reinforcing bar sizes, and the details for placing the reinforcing bars. It is also a good practice for the engineer to visit the job site during the construc-

Table 2. Concrete Reinforcing Steel Bar Sizes and Dimensions

Deformed-bar designation	Weight, lb. per ft.	Diameter, in.	Cross-section area, sq. in.	Perimeter, in.	Max. outside dia., in.
#2	0.167	0.250	0.05	0.786	
#3	0.376	0.375	0.11	1.178	7⁄16
#4	0.668	0.500	0.20	1.571	9⁄16
#5	1.043	0.625	0.31	1.963	11⁄16
#6	1.502	0.750	0.44	2.356	7⁄8
#7	2.044	0.875	0.60	2.749	1
#8	2.670	1.000	0.79	3.142	1⅛
#9	3.400	1.128	1.00	3.544	1¼
#10	4.303	1.270	1.27	3.990	1⁷⁄16
#11	5.313	1.410	1.56	4.430	1⅝
#14	7.65	1.693	2.25	5.32	1¹⁵⁄16
#18	13.60	2.257	4.00	7.09	2½

tion to inspect the accuracy of the placing of the reinforcing steel. The A.C.I. Specification for Structural Concrete for Buildings No. 301-84 recommends allowable fabrication and placing tolerances for reinforcement. The bars should be wired together and secured in place to prevent any movement that may be caused by placing the concrete. Galvanized metal or concrete block bar chairs are used to support the reinforcement in the forms to obtain the required concrete cover. In no instance should these chairs be used to support form boards or construction loads other than the weight of the reinforcing bars. Table 3 gives the recom-

mended concrete cover for reinforcing bars in the various structural members. Table 4 gives the recommended clear distances between reinforcing bars.

Reinforcing bars can be connected either by a lapped splice or by a butt-welded connection. Splices should not be made at points of critical stress in the member, or at points which are not specified on the working drawings, without the authorization of the design engineer. Lapped splices acting in tension or compression should not be made with rein-

Table 3. Minimum Clear Cover of Concrete for Reinforcing Steel

Location of reinforcement in concrete	Clear distance
Reinforcement in footings and other structural members in which the concrete is poured directly against the ground	3″
Formed concrete surfaces to be exposed to weather or in contact with the ground for bar sizes greater than #5	2″
Formed concrete surfaces to be exposed to weather or in contact with the ground for bar sizes #5 or less	1½″
Slabs and walls not exposed to weather or in contact with the ground	¾″
Beams and girders not exposed to weather or in contact with the ground	1½″
Floor joists with a maximum clear spacing of 30″	¾″
Column spirals or ties (not less than 1½ times the maximum size of the coarse aggregate or . . .)	1½″

Note: Except for concrete slabs or joists, the concrete cover protection shall not be less than the nominal diameter of the reinforcing bar.

Table 4. Minimum Clear Spacing Distance between Reinforcing Bars

Space between bars	Clear distance
Clear distance between parallel bars except in columns and layers of bars in beams and girders	Not less than the nominal diameter of the bars, or 1⅓ times the size of the coarse aggregate, or not less than 1″
Clear distance between layers of reinforcement in beams or girders; the bars in each layer shall be directly above and below the bars in the adjacent layer	Not less than 1″
Clear distance between bars in walls and slabs	Not more than three times the wall or slab thickness or more than 18″
Clear distance between bars in spirally reinforced and tied columns	1½ times the nominal bar diameter, 1½ times the maximum size of the coarse aggregate, or not less than 1½″

Note: The clear distances above also apply for the clear distances between contact splices and adjacent splices of reinforcing bars.

forcing bars larger in size than #11. If deformed reinforcing bars are used and $f'_c = 3000$ psi, the recommended length of lap in a splice is as follows: tension splices, not less than 24, 30, and 36 bar diameters for specified yield strengths of 40,000, 50,000 and 60,000 psi, respectively; compression splices, not less than 24, 30, and 36 bar diameters for specified yield strengths of 40,000, 50,000, and 60,000 psi, respectively. These bar diameter lengths should be doubled for plain reinforcing bars and increased by $\frac{1}{3}$ for f'_c less than 3000 psi. The minimum length of lap should not be less than 1'0". Welded splices are usually made for large size reinforcing bars. This is done by butt welding the square cut ends together so that the connection is capable of resisting 125% of the specified yield strength of the bar in tension. Various mechanical bar connectors are available; however, their use would depend upon the approval of the engineer and their acceptability by the design criteria.

The preceding information is only a brief description of some of the aspects of reinforced concrete when it is used as a construction material. The design, construction, and quality control of reinforced concrete is a very complex field. This material is presented as a guide for the use of the structural details in this volume. The American Concrete Institute and the Portland Cement Association have compiled a large amount of information on many subjects that are concerned with reinforced concrete construction. These standards are subject to revision whenever the studies of the committees responsible indicate that developments in concrete design and construction warrant any change. Working drawings are made to communicate the design requirements and configurations to the contractor. These drawings should be supplemented by shop drawings of the individual reinforcing bars and their method of placement. The accuracy of design, the quality of workmanship, and the quality control of the construction materials are important factors in reinforced concrete design and construction. Once the reinforcing steel and the concrete are finally placed, a total commitment is made by the engineer, the job-site inspector, the laboratory testing the materials, and the contractor. The owner of the building must be able to rely on the responsibility of this commitment. Responsibility of construction must follow progressively and in sequence from the design engineer to the contractor.

DETAILS

Notes ▪ Drawings ▪ Ideas

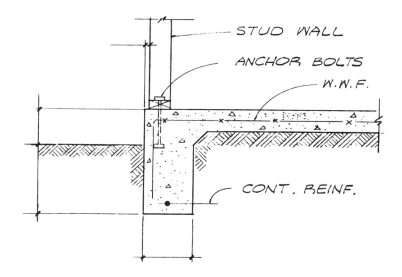

Detail 1(a). A section of a continuous concrete footing for an exterior wood stud wall. The stud wall is set back to allow the exterior wall covering to meet the face of the concrete. The depth and width of the footing depend on the soil conditions.

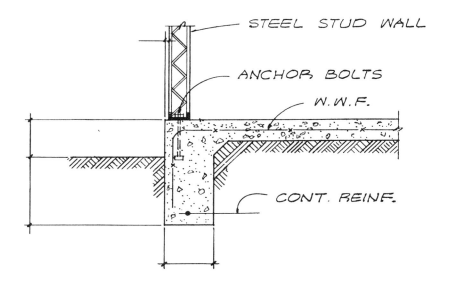

Detail 1(b). A section of a continuous concrete footing for an exterior steel stud wall. The stud wall is set back to allow the exterior wall covering to meet the face of the concrete. The depth and width of the footing depend on the soil conditions.

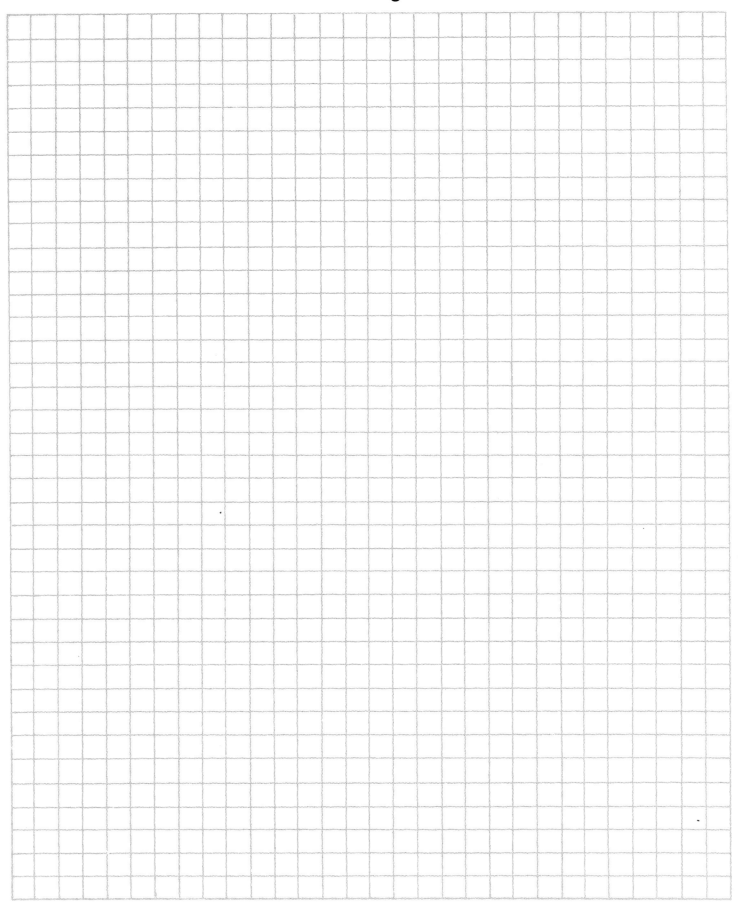

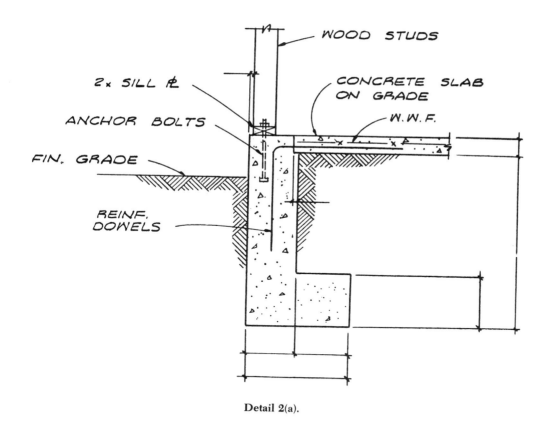

WOOD STUDS

2x SILL ℞

ANCHOR BOLTS

CONCRETE SLAB ON GRADE

W.W.F.

FIN. GRADE

REINF. DOWELS

Detail 2(a).

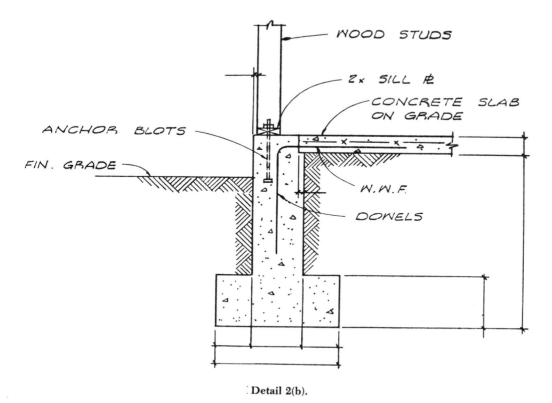

WOOD STUDS

2x SILL ℞

ANCHOR BLOTS

CONCRETE SLAB ON GRADE

FIN. GRADE

W.W.F.

DOWELS

Detail 2(b).

Detail 2(a) and (b). A section of a continuous concrete footing for an exterior wood stud wall. The footing is connected to the slab on grade by reinforcing dowels. The stud wall is set back to allow the exterior wall covering to meet the face of the concrete. The depth and width of the footing depend on the soil conditions.

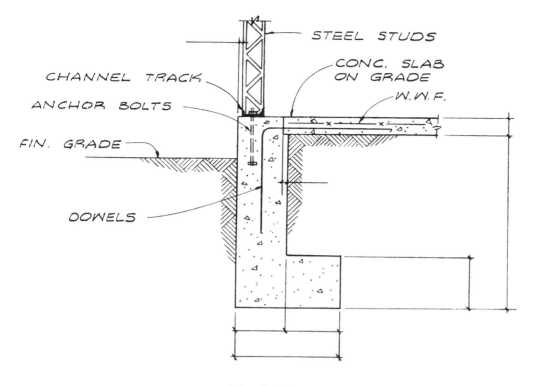

STEEL STUDS

CONC. SLAB
ON GRADE

W.W.F.

CHANNEL TRACK

ANCHOR BOLTS

FIN. GRADE

DOWELS

| Detail 3(a).

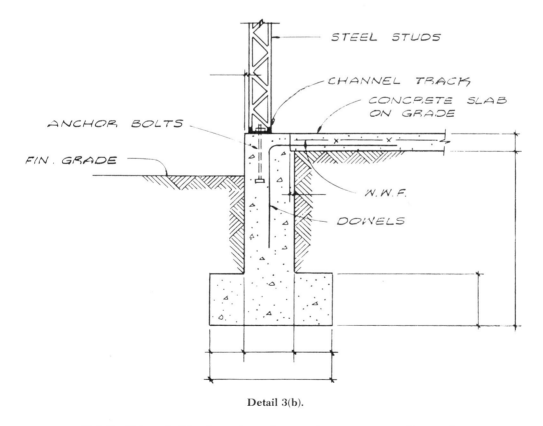

STEEL STUDS

CHANNEL TRACK

CONCRETE SLAB
ON GRADE

ANCHOR BOLTS

FIN. GRADE

W.W.F.

DOWELS

Detail 3(b).

Details 3(a) and (b). A section of a continuous concrete footing for an exterior steel stud wall. The footing is connected to the slab on grade with reinforcing dowels. The steel studs are set back to allow the exterior wall covering to meet the face of the concrete. The depth and width of the footing depend on the soil conditions.

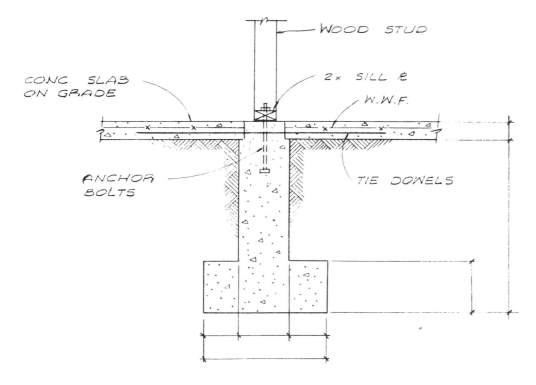

Detail 4. A section of a continuous concrete footing for an interior wood stud wall. The concrete slab on grade is connected across the top of the footing by reinforcing dowels. The depth and width of the footing depend on the soil conditions.

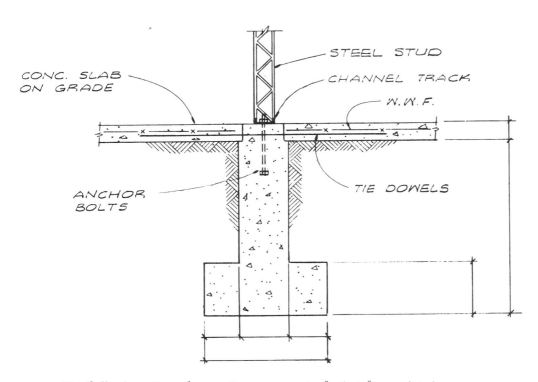

Detail 5. A section of a continuous concrete footing for an interior steel stud wall. The concrete slab on grade is connected across the top of the footing by reinforcing dowels. The depth and width of the footing depend on the soil conditions.

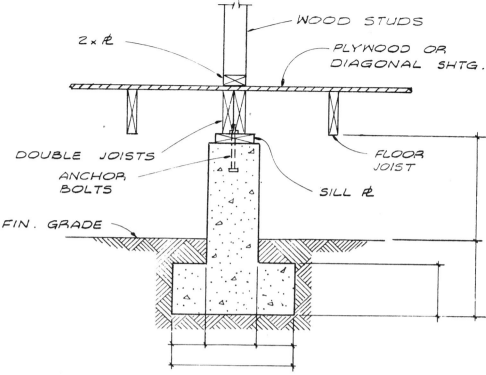

Detail 6. A section of a continuous concrete footing for an interior wood stud wall. The floor joists span parallel to the footing. The weight of the wall is transferred to the concrete footing by the double joists. The clear distance between the finished grade and the bottom of the floor joists is determined by the local building code. The depth and width of the footing depend on the soil conditions.

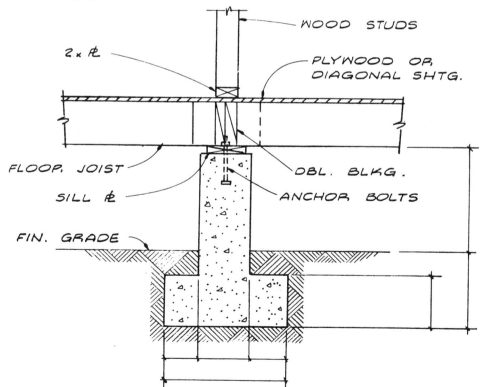

Detail 7. A section of a continuous concrete footing for an interior wood stud wall and floor joists. The floor joists are lapped and nailed together. The distance between the bottom of the floor joists and the finished grade is determined by the local building code. The depth and width of the footing depend on the soil conditions.

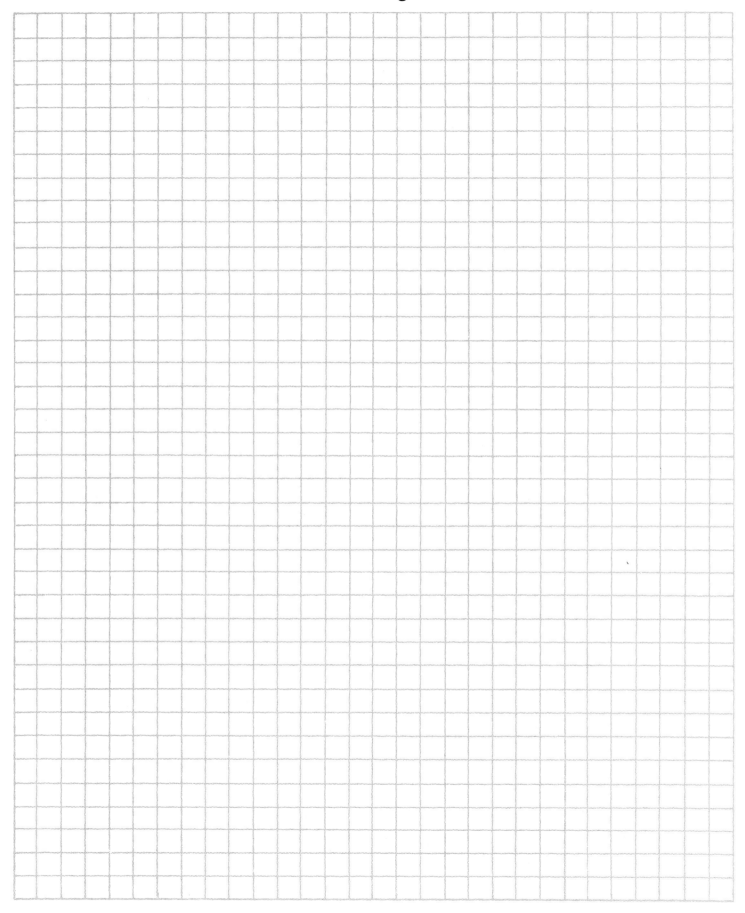

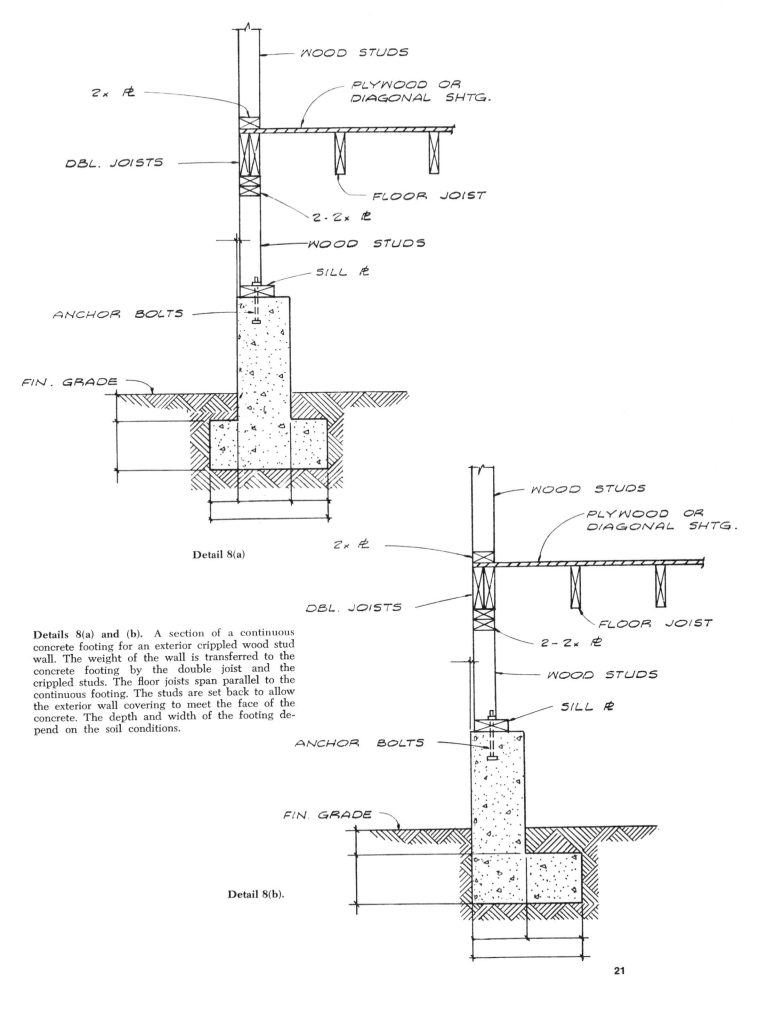

WOOD STUDS

PLYWOOD OR DIAGONAL SHTG.

2× R̶

DBL. JOISTS

FLOOR JOIST

2-2× R̶

WOOD STUDS

SILL R̶

ANCHOR BOLTS

FIN. GRADE

Detail 8(a)

Details 8(a) and (b). A section of a continuous concrete footing for an exterior crippled wood stud wall. The weight of the wall is transferred to the concrete footing by the double joist and the crippled studs. The floor joists span parallel to the continuous footing. The studs are set back to allow the exterior wall covering to meet the face of the concrete. The depth and width of the footing depend on the soil conditions.

WOOD STUDS

PLYWOOD OR DIAGONAL SHTG.

2× R̶

DBL. JOISTS

FLOOR JOIST

2-2× R̶

WOOD STUDS

SILL R̶

ANCHOR BOLTS

FIN. GRADE

Detail 8(b).

21

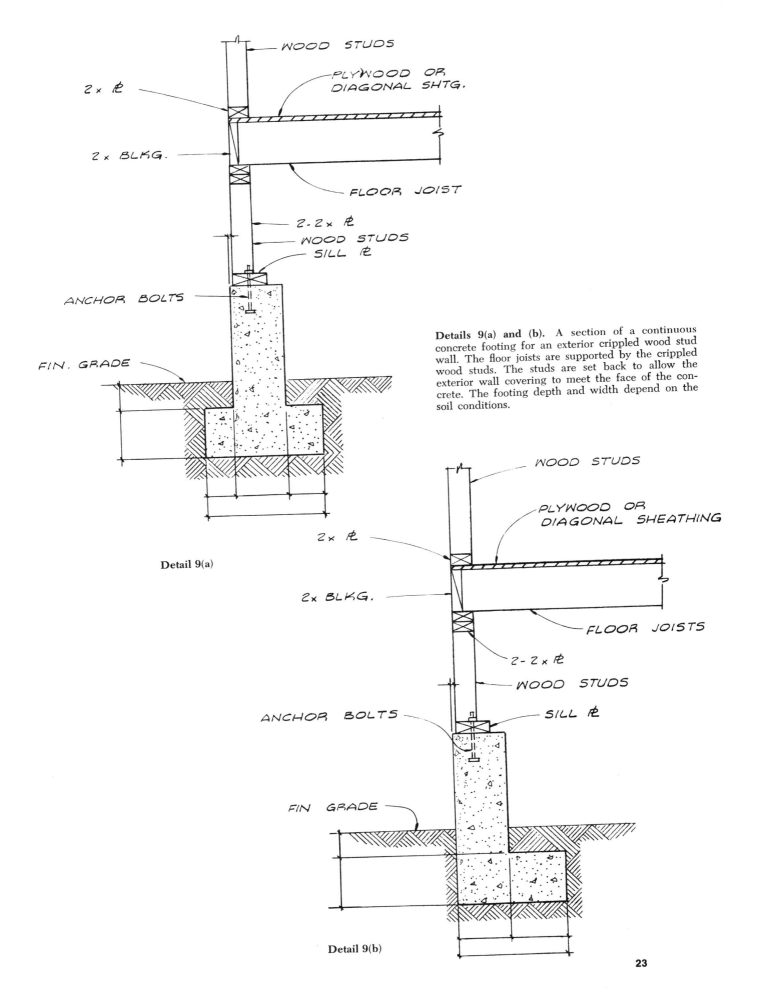

WOOD STUDS

PLYWOOD OR
DIAGONAL SHTG.

2 x ₽

2 x BLKG.

FLOOR JOIST

2-2x ₽

WOOD STUDS
SILL ₽

ANCHOR BOLTS

FIN. GRADE

Details 9(a) and (b). A section of a continuous concrete footing for an exterior crippled wood stud wall. The floor joists are supported by the crippled wood studs. The studs are set back to allow the exterior wall covering to meet the face of the concrete. The footing depth and width depend on the soil conditions.

Detail 9(a)

WOOD STUDS

PLYWOOD OR
DIAGONAL SHEATHING

2 x ₽

2x BLKG.

FLOOR JOISTS

2-2 x ₽

WOOD STUDS

ANCHOR BOLTS

SILL ₽

FIN GRADE

Detail 9(b)

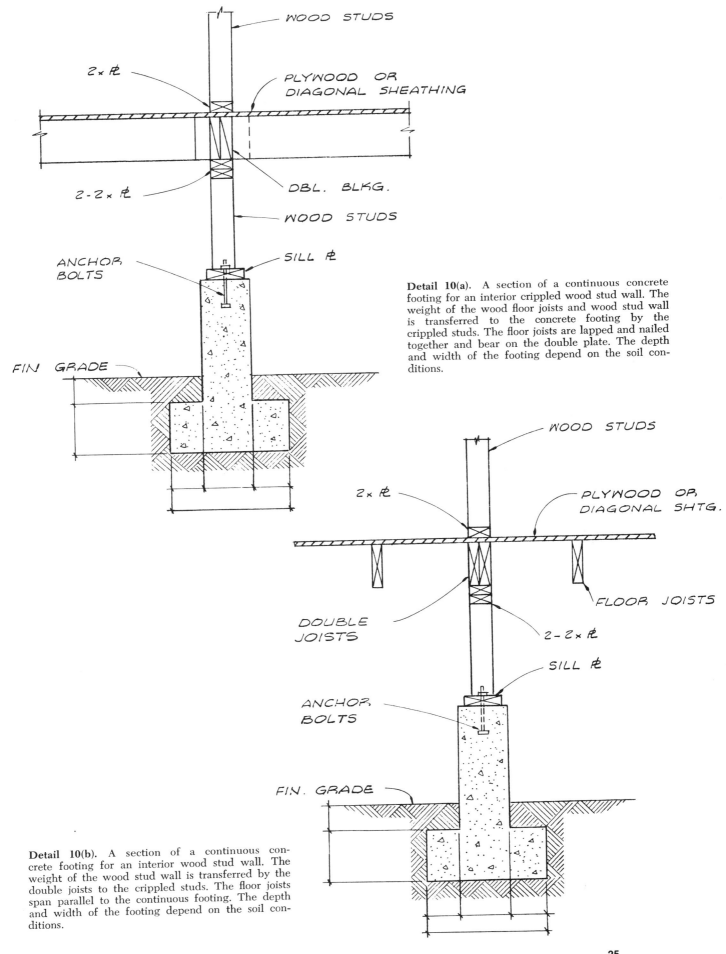

WOOD STUDS

2 x ℔

PLYWOOD OR
DIAGONAL SHEATHING

2-2 x ℔

DBL. BLKG.

WOOD STUDS

ANCHOR
BOLTS

SILL ℔

FIN GRADE

Detail 10(a). A section of a continuous concrete footing for an interior crippled wood stud wall. The weight of the wood floor joists and wood stud wall is transferred to the concrete footing by the crippled studs. The floor joists are lapped and nailed together and bear on the double plate. The depth and width of the footing depend on the soil conditions.

WOOD STUDS

2 x ℔

PLYWOOD OR
DIAGONAL SHTG.

FLOOR JOISTS

DOUBLE
JOISTS

2-2 x ℔

SILL ℔

ANCHOR
BOLTS

FIN. GRADE

Detail 10(b). A section of a continuous concrete footing for an interior wood stud wall. The weight of the wood stud wall is transferred by the double joists to the crippled studs. The floor joists span parallel to the continuous footing. The depth and width of the footing depend on the soil conditions.

Notes ▪ Drawings ▪ Ideas

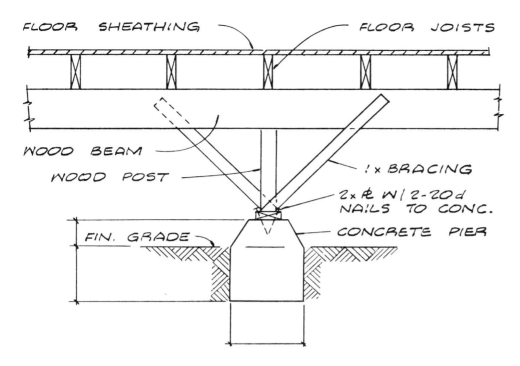

FLOOR SHEATHING   FLOOR JOISTS

WOOD BEAM

WOOD POST

FIN. GRADE

1 x BRACING

2 x ₤ W/ 2-20d NAILS TO CONC.

CONCRETE PIER

Detail 11(a). An elevation of wood floor joists and beams supported over the finished grade. The depth and size of the supporting concrete pier depend on the soil conditions. See Detail 11(b).

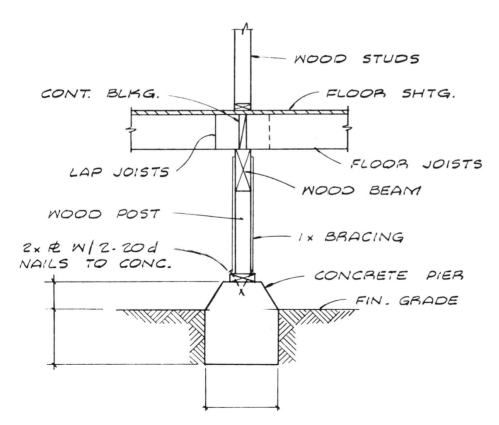

WOOD STUDS

CONT. BLKG.   FLOOR SHTG.

LAP JOISTS

FLOOR JOISTS

WOOD BEAM

WOOD POST

1 x BRACING

2 x ₤ W/ 2-20d NAILS TO CONC.

CONCRETE PIER

FIN. GRADE

Detail 11(b). A section of Detail 11(a). The floor joists lap over the wood beam and are nailed together. The 1"-wide diagonal braces on each side of the wood post restrain the floor laterally. The bracing may be omitted if the posts are short and the floor is laterally restrained by a continuous footing.

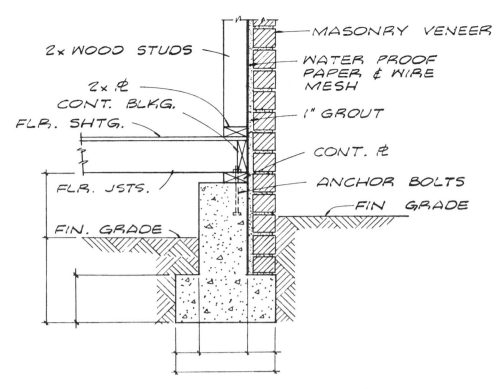

2x WOOD STUDS

2x ℓ
CONT. BLKG.
FLR. SHTG.

FLR. JSTS.

FIN. GRADE

MASONRY VENEER

WATER PROOF PAPER & WIRE MESH

1" GROUT

CONT. ℓ

ANCHOR BOLTS

FIN GRADE

Detail 12(a). A section of a continuous concrete footing for an exterior wood stud wall with an exterior masonry veneer surface. The floor joists bear on the sill plate. The distance between the finished grade and the bottom of the floor joists is determined by the local building code. The masonry veneer is connected to the wood studs as shown. The depth and width of the footing depend on the soil conditions.

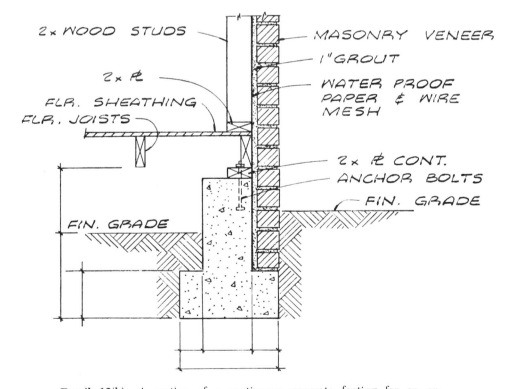

2x WOOD STUDS

2x ℓ
FLR. SHEATHING
FLR. JOISTS

FIN. GRADE

MASONRY VENEER

1" GROUT

WATER PROOF PAPER & WIRE MESH

2x ℓ CONT.
ANCHOR BOLTS

FIN. GRADE

Detail 12(b). A section of a continuous concrete footing for an exterior wood stud wall with an exterior masonry veneer surface. The floor joists span parallel to the wall. The double joist transfers the weight of the wall to the continuous footing. The distance between the finished grade and the bottom of the floor joists is determined by the local building code. The masonry veneer is connected to the wood studs as shown. The depth and width of the footing depend on the soil conditions.

Notes · Drawings · Ideas

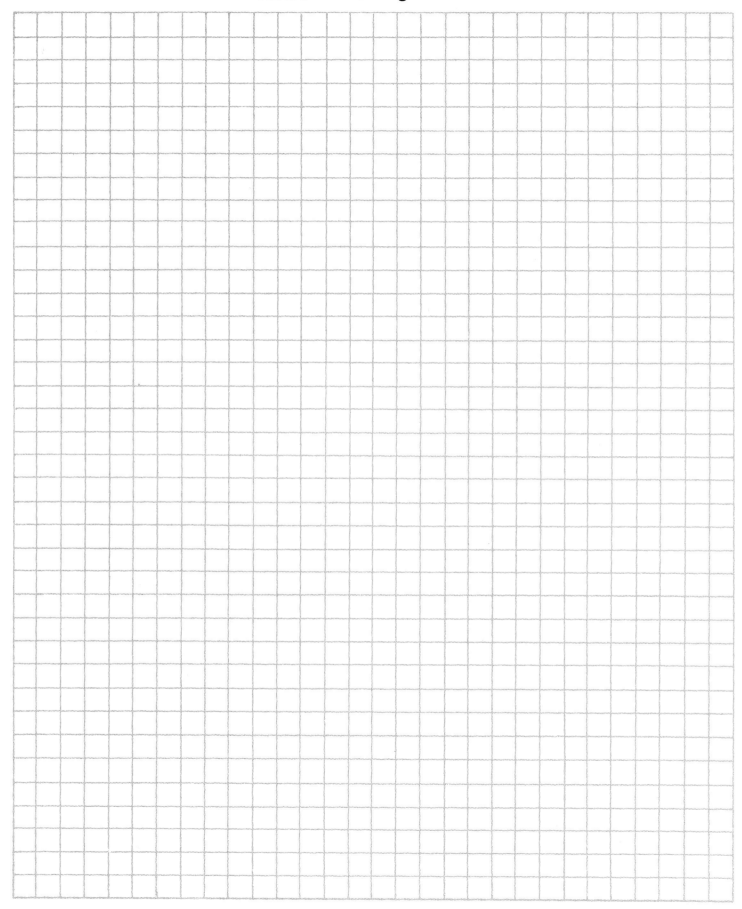

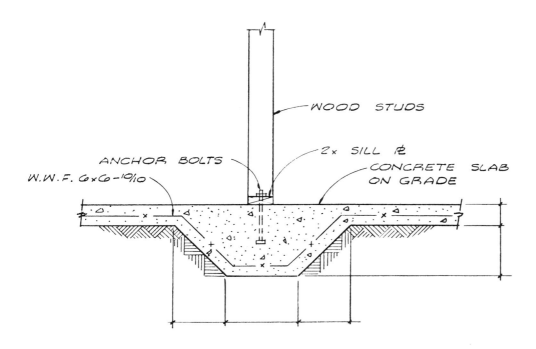

WOOD STUDS

ANCHOR BOLTS

2× SILL ℞

CONCRETE SLAB
ON GRADE

W.W.F. 6×6 - ¹⁰/₁₀

Detail 13(a). A section of a non-bearing wood stud wall on a concrete slab on grade. The increased width and depth of the concrete slab depend on the soil conditions.

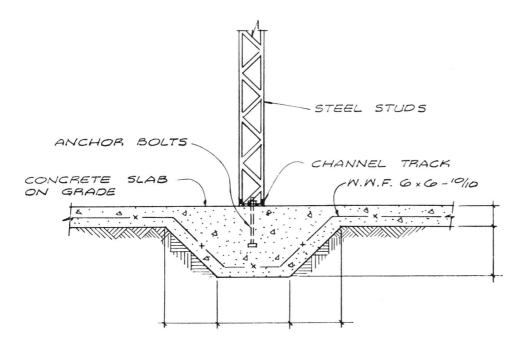

STEEL STUDS

ANCHOR BOLTS

CHANNEL TRACK

CONCRETE SLAB
ON GRADE

W.W.F. 6×6 - ¹⁰/₁₀

Detail 13(b). A section of a non-bearing steel stud wall on a concrete slab on grade. The increased width and depth of the concrete slab depend on the soil conditions.

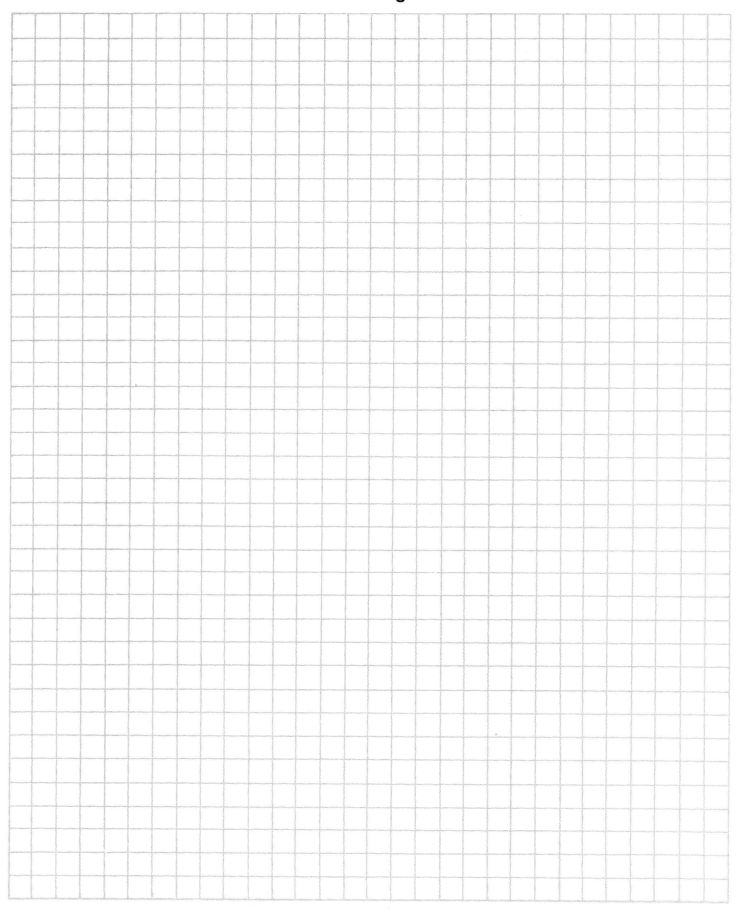

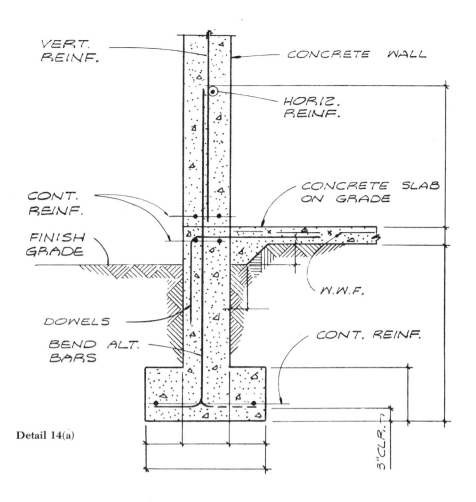

VERT. REINF.

CONCRETE WALL

HORIZ. REINF.

CONCRETE SLAB ON GRADE

CONT. REINF.

FINISH GRADE

W.W.F.

DOWELS

BEND ALT. BARS

CONT. REINF.

3" CLR.

Detail 14(a)

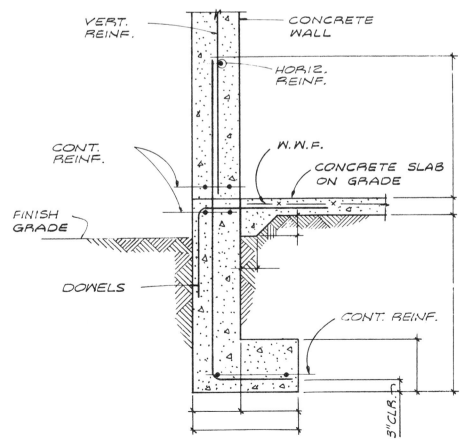

VERT. REINF.

CONCRETE WALL

HORIZ. REINF.

W.W.F.

CONCRETE SLAB ON GRADE

CONT. REINF.

FINISH GRADE

DOWELS

CONT. REINF.

3" CLR.

Detail 14(b)

Details 14(a) and (b). A section of a continuous concrete footing for an exterior concrete wall. The footing is connected to the concrete slab on grade and to the concrete wall above grade by reinforcing dowels. The reinforcing dowels lap the wall vertical reinforcement 40 bar diameters or not less than 24″. The size and spacing of the reinforcing steel are determined by calculation. The depth and width of the footing depend on the soil conditions.

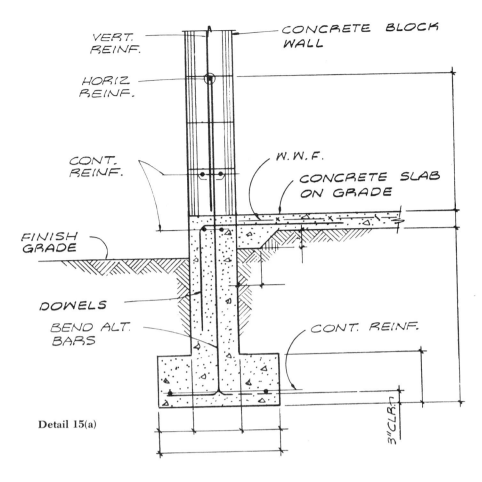

VERT. REINF.

CONCRETE BLOCK WALL

HORIZ. REINF.

W.W.F.

CONCRETE SLAB ON GRADE

CONT. REINF.

FINISH GRADE

DOWELS

BEND ALT. BARS

CONT. REINF.

3"CLR.

Detail 15(a)

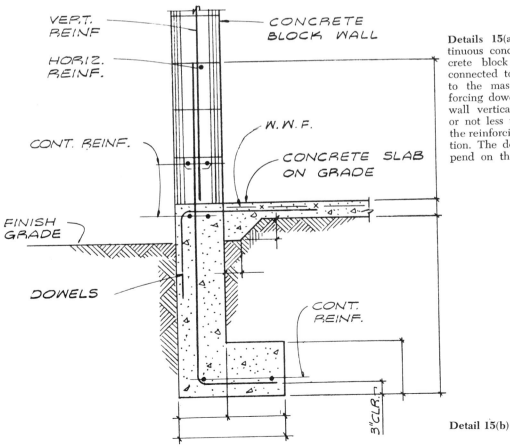

VERT. REINF

CONCRETE BLOCK WALL

HORIZ. REINF.

CONT. REINF.

W.W.F.

CONCRETE SLAB ON GRADE

FINISH GRADE

DOWELS

CONT. REINF.

3"CLR.

Detail 15(b)

Details 15(a) and (b). A section of a continuous concrete footing and an exterior concrete block masonry wall. The footing is connected to the concrete slab on grade and to the masonry wall above grade by reinforcing dowels. The reinforcing dowels lap the wall vertical reinforcement 30 bar diameters or not less than 24″. The size and spacing of the reinforcing steel are determined by calculation. The depth and width of the footing depend on the soil conditions.

Notes ▪ Drawings ▪ Ideas

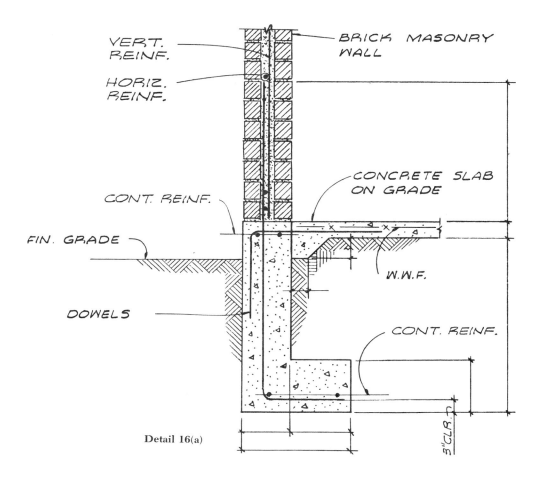

VERT. REINF.

HORIZ. REINF.

BRICK MASONRY WALL

CONT. REINF.

CONCRETE SLAB ON GRADE

FIN. GRADE

W.W.F.

DOWELS

CONT. REINF.

3" CLR.

Detail 16(a)

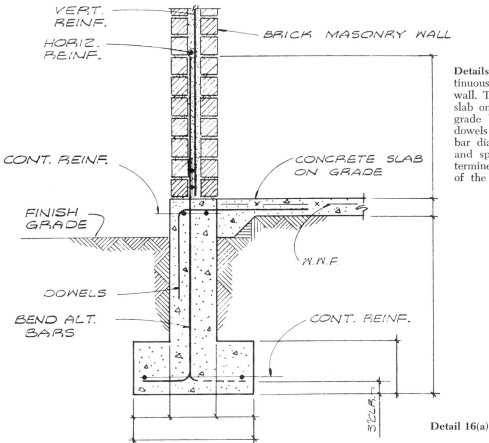

VERT. REINF.

HORIZ. REINF.

BRICK MASONRY WALL

CONT. REINF.

CONCRETE SLAB ON GRADE

FINISH GRADE

W.W.F.

DOWELS

BEND ALT. BARS

CONT. REINF.

3" CLR.

Detail 16(a)

Details 16(a) and (b). A section of a continuous concrete footing and an exterior brick wall. The footing is connected to the concrete slab on grade and to the masonry wall above grade by reinforcing dowels. The reinforcing dowels lap the wall vertical reinforcement 30 bar diameters or not less than 24″. The size and spacing of the reinforcing steel are determined by calculation. The depth and width of the footing depend on the soil conditions.

Notes ▪ Drawings ▪ Ideas

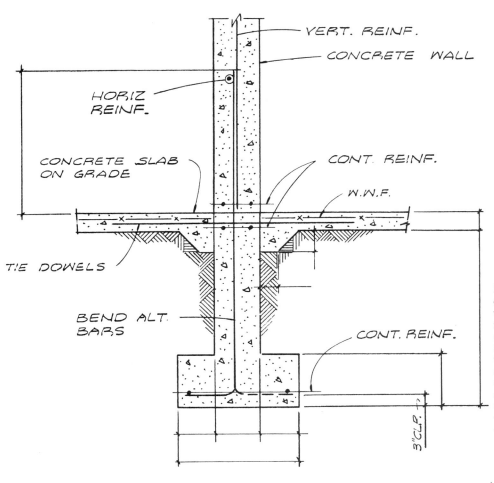

VERT. REINF.

CONCRETE WALL

HORIZ REINF.

CONCRETE SLAB ON GRADE

CONT. REINF.

W.W.F.

TIE DOWELS

BEND ALT. BARS

CONT. REINF.

3" CLR.

Detail 17(a). A section of a continuous concrete footing and an interior concrete wall. The concrete slab on grade is connected across the top of the footing by reinforcing dowels. The footing is connected to the concrete wall above grade with reinforcing dowels. The reinforcing dowels lap the wall vertical reinforcement 40 bar diameters or not less than 24″. The size and spacing of the reinforcing steel are determined by calculation. The depth and width of the footing depend on the soil conditions.

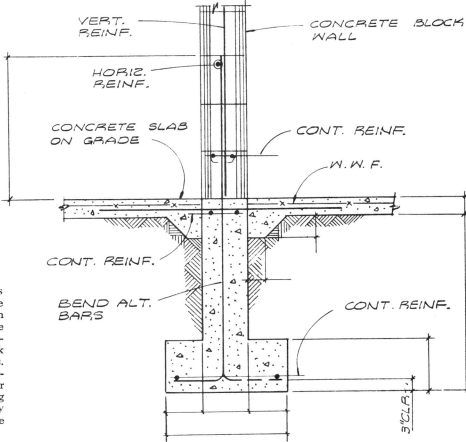

VERT. REINF.

CONCRETE BLOCK WALL

HORIZ. REINF.

CONCRETE SLAB ON GRADE

CONT. REINF.

W.W.F.

CONT. REINF.

BEND ALT. BARS

CONT. REINF.

3" CLR.

Detail 17(b). A section of a continuous concrete footing and an interior concrete block masonry wall. The concrete slab on grade is connected across the top of the footing with reinforcing dowels. The footing is connected to the concrete block wall above grade with reinforcing dowels. The reinforcing dowels lap the wall vertical reinforcement 30 bar diameters or not less than 24″. The size and spacing of the reinforcing steel are determined by calculation. The depth and width of the footing depend on the soil conditions.

Notes ▪ Drawings ▪ Ideas

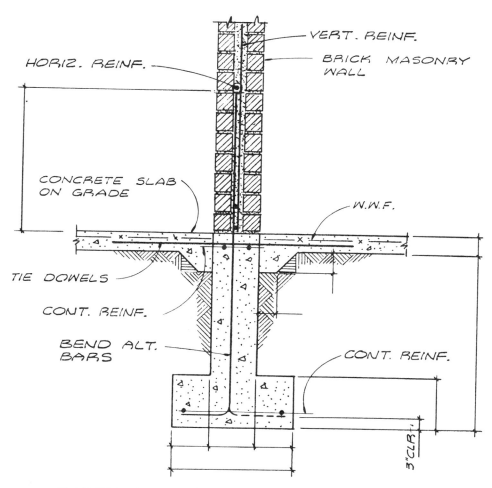

Detail 17(c). A section of a continuous concrete footing and an interior brick wall. The concrete slab on grade is connected across the top of the footing with reinforcing dowels. The footing is connected to the brick wall above grade with reinforcing dowels. The reinforcing dowels lap the wall vertical reinforcement 30 bar diameters or not less than 24". The size and spacing of the reinforcing steel are determined by calculation. The depth and width of the footing depend on the soil condition.

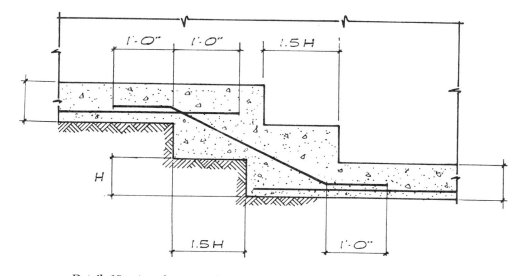

Detail 18. An elevation of a stepped continuous footing. The length of the run of the step is 1½ times the height of the rise of the step. The footing reinforcing bars are lapped in accordance with the local building code.

Notes ▪ Drawings ▪ Ideas

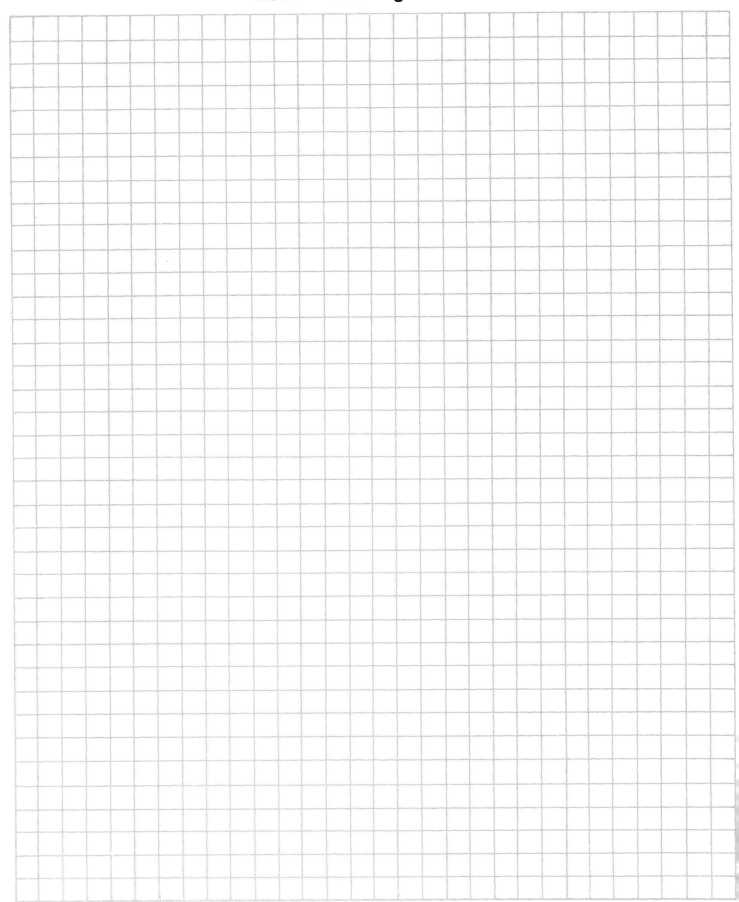

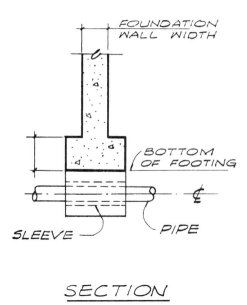

SECTION

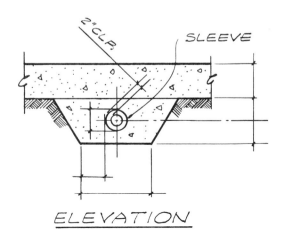

ELEVATION

Detail 19(a). A section showing a steel pipe passing through and below a continuous concrete footing. The pipe is sleeved to prevent damage caused by possible footing deflection. An additional depth and width of concrete covers the pipe sleeve and allows sufficient bearing of the continuous footing. See Detail 19(b).

Detail 19(b). A section of Detail 19(a).

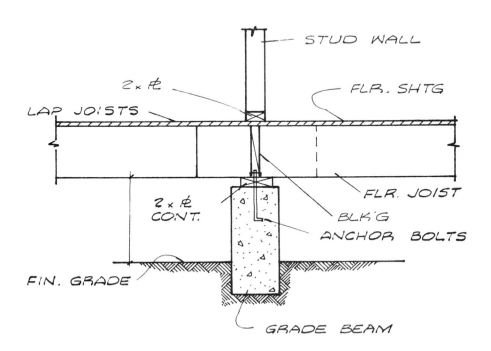

Detail 20. A section of a concrete grade beam supporting an interior wood stud wall and floor joists. The floor joists are lapped and nailed together. The reinforcing steel in the grade beam is not shown. The distance between the finished grade and the bottom of the floor joists is determined by the local building code.

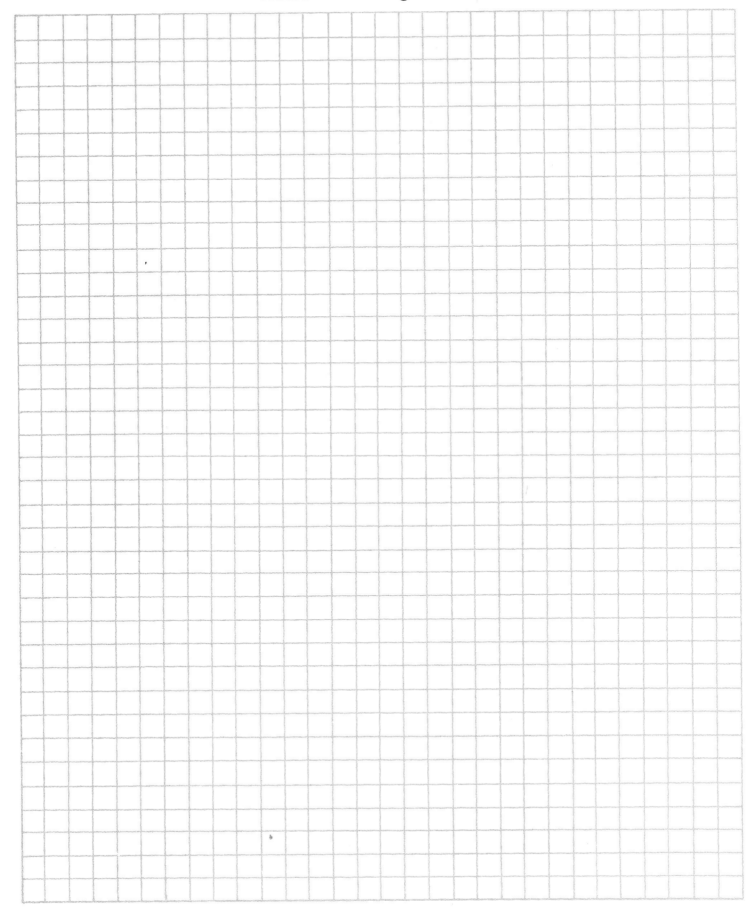

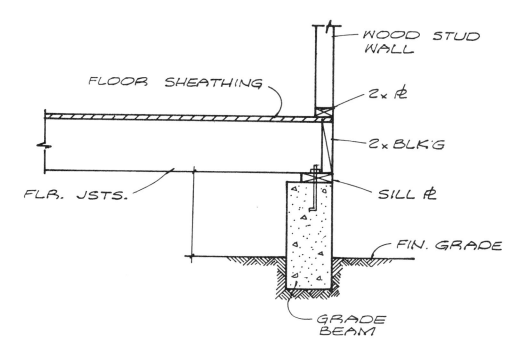

Detail 21(a). A section of a concrete grade beam supporting an exterior wood stud wall and floor joists. The reinforcing steel in the grade beam is not shown. The distance between finished grade and the bottom of the floor joists is determined by the local building code.

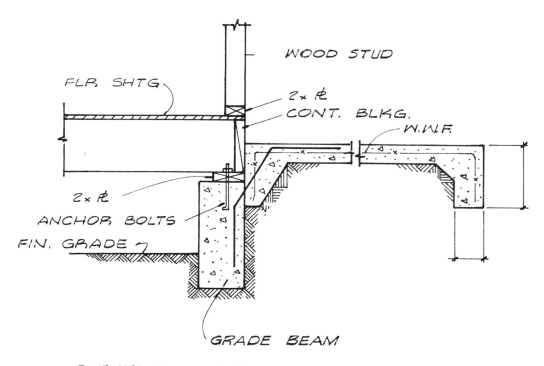

Detail 21(b). A section of a concrete grade beam supporting an exterior wood stud wall and floor joists. The reinforcing steel in the grade beam is not shown. The distance between finished grade and the bottom of the floor joists is determined by the local building code. The exterior concrete slab on grade is connected to the grade beam by reinforcing dowels as shown.

Notes · Drawings · Ideas

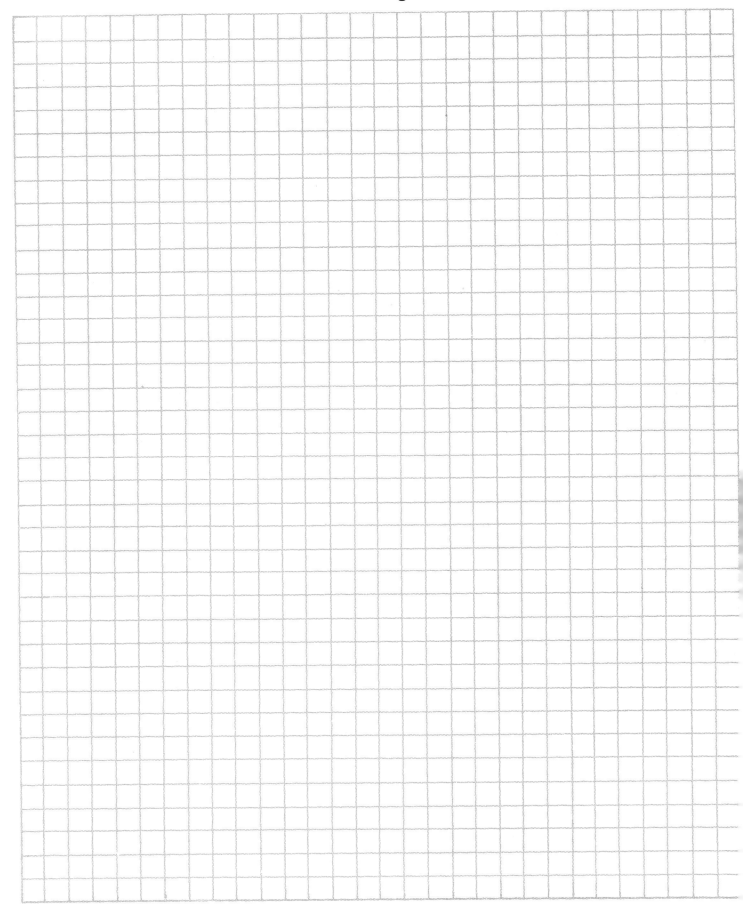

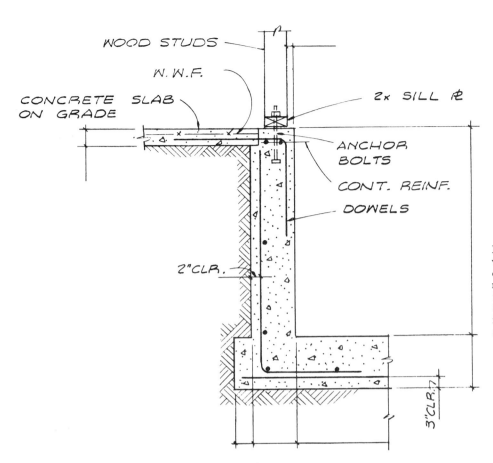

WOOD STUDS

W.W.F.

CONCRETE SLAB
ON GRADE

2x SILL ℞

ANCHOR
BOLTS

CONT. REINF.

DOWELS

2"CLR.

3"CLR.

Detail 22(a). A section of a concrete pit wall and a wood stud wall. The pit wall is connected to the concrete slab on grade with reinforcing dowels. The stud wall is set back to allow the wall covering to meet the face of the concrete. The size and spacing of the reinforcing steel in the pit wall and the footing are determined by calculation.

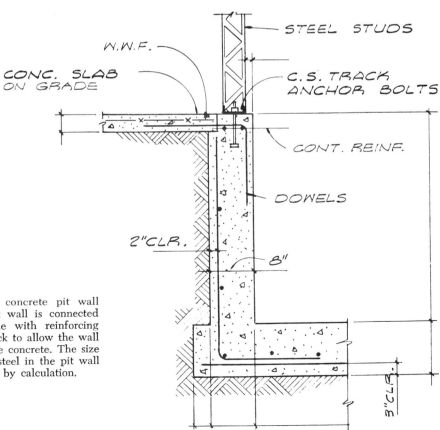

STEEL STUDS

W.W.F.

CONC. SLAB
ON GRADE

C.S. TRACK
ANCHOR BOLTS

CONT. REINF.

DOWELS

2"CLR.

8"

3"CLR.

Detail 22(b). A section of a concrete pit wall and a steel stud wall. The pit wall is connected to the concrete slab on grade with reinforcing dowels. The stud wall is set back to allow the wall covering to meet the face of the concrete. The size and spacing of the reinforcing steel in the pit wall and the footing are determined by calculation.

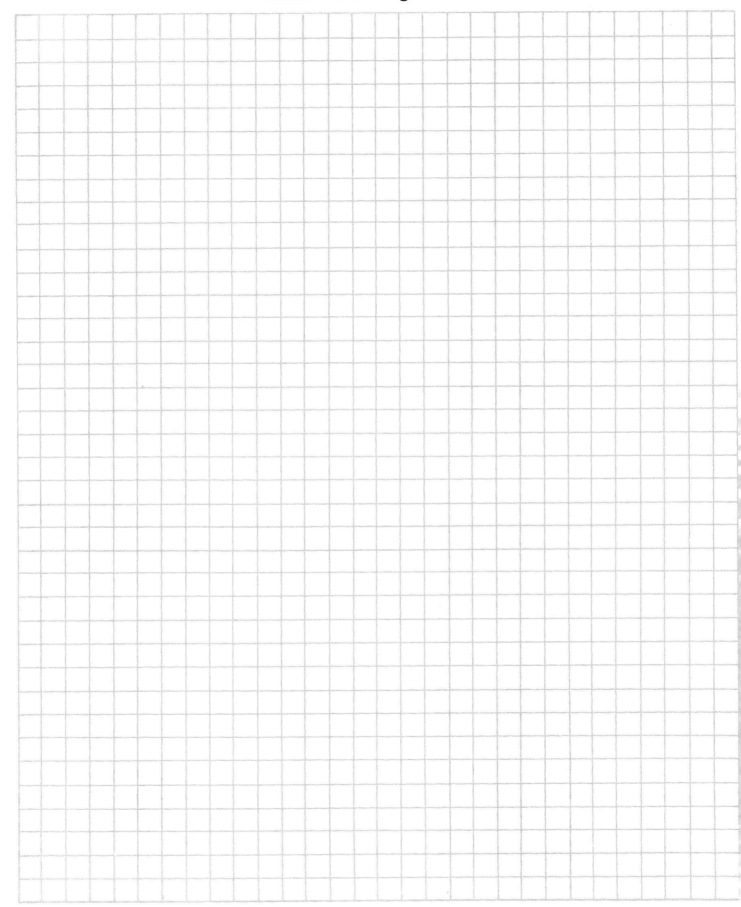

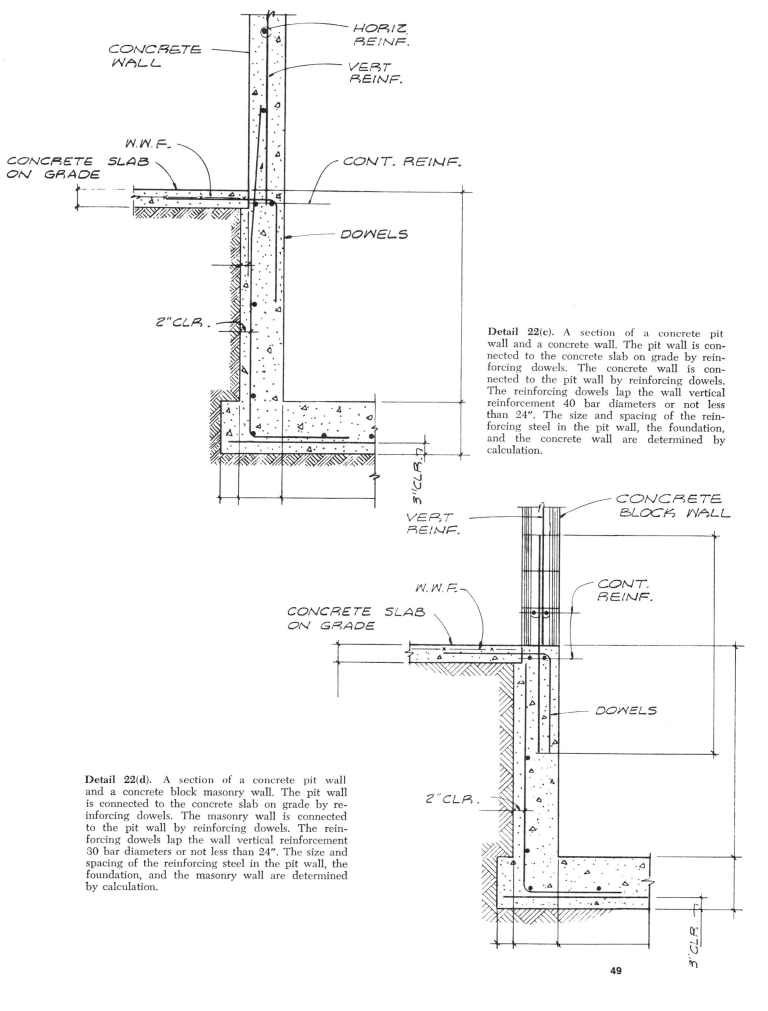

CONCRETE WALL

HORIZ. REINF.

VERT. REINF.

W.W.F.

CONCRETE SLAB ON GRADE

CONT. REINF.

DOWELS

2"CLR.

3"CLR.

Detail 22(c). A section of a concrete pit wall and a concrete wall. The pit wall is connected to the concrete slab on grade by reinforcing dowels. The concrete wall is connected to the pit wall by reinforcing dowels. The reinforcing dowels lap the wall vertical reinforcement 40 bar diameters or not less than 24″. The size and spacing of the reinforcing steel in the pit wall, the foundation, and the concrete wall are determined by calculation.

VERT. REINF.

CONCRETE BLOCK WALL

W.W.F.

CONCRETE SLAB ON GRADE

CONT. REINF.

DOWELS

2"CLR.

3"CLR.

Detail 22(d). A section of a concrete pit wall and a concrete block masonry wall. The pit wall is connected to the concrete slab on grade by reinforcing dowels. The masonry wall is connected to the pit wall by reinforcing dowels. The reinforcing dowels lap the wall vertical reinforcement 30 bar diameters or not less than 24″. The size and spacing of the reinforcing steel in the pit wall, the foundation, and the masonry wall are determined by calculation.

49

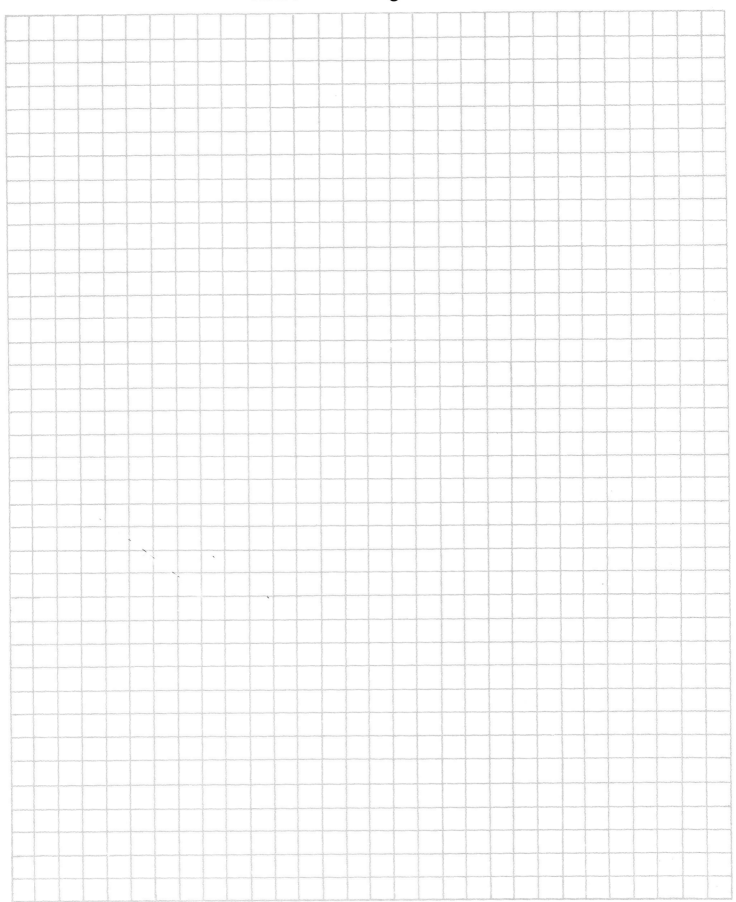

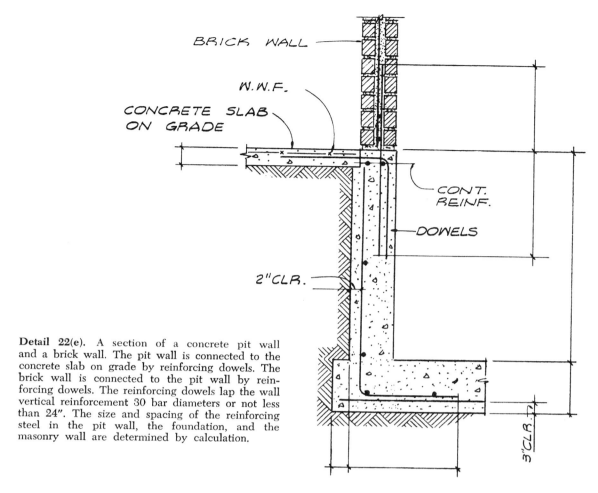

BRICK WALL

W.W.F.

CONCRETE SLAB ON GRADE

CONT. REINF.

DOWELS

2"CLR.

3"CLR.

Detail 22(e). A section of a concrete pit wall and a brick wall. The pit wall is connected to the concrete slab on grade by reinforcing dowels. The brick wall is connected to the pit wall by reinforcing dowels. The reinforcing dowels lap the wall vertical reinforcement 30 bar diameters or not less than 24″. The size and spacing of the reinforcing steel in the pit wall, the foundation, and the masonry wall are determined by calculation.

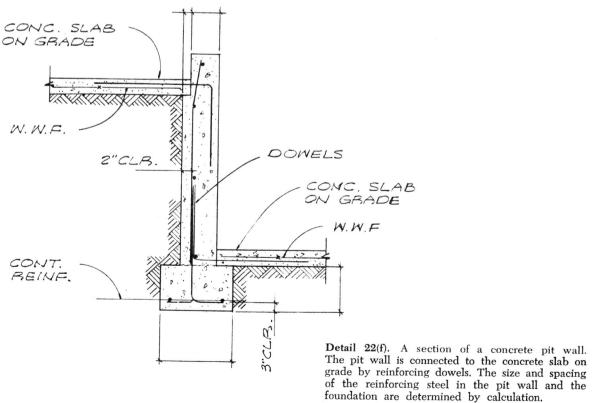

CONC. SLAB ON GRADE

W.W.F.

2"CLR.

DOWELS

CONC. SLAB ON GRADE

W.W.F

CONT. REINF.

3"CLR.

Detail 22(f). A section of a concrete pit wall. The pit wall is connected to the concrete slab on grade by reinforcing dowels. The size and spacing of the reinforcing steel in the pit wall and the foundation are determined by calculation.

Notes ▪ Drawings ▪ Ideas

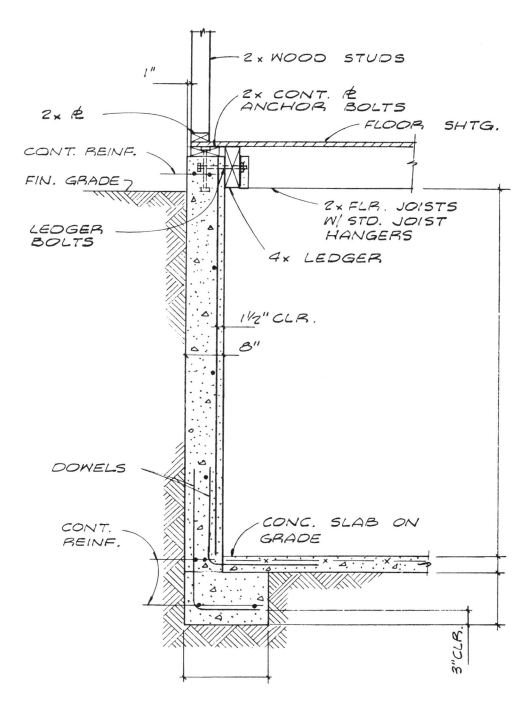

1"

2x ₵

CONT. REINF.

FIN. GRADE

LEDGER
BOLTS

DOWELS

CONT.
REINF.

2x WOOD STUDS

2x CONT. ₵
ANCHOR BOLTS

FLOOR SHTG.

2x FLR. JOISTS
W/ STD. JOIST
HANGERS

4x LEDGER

1½" CLR.

8"

CONC. SLAB ON
GRADE

3" CLR.

Detail 23(a). A section of a concrete basement wall supporting wood floor joists and an exterior wood stud wall. The stud wall is set back to allow the exterior wall covering to meet the face of the concrete. The floor joists are connected to a 4" wide wood ledger by joist hangers. The ledger is bolted to the wall. The size and spacing of the ledger bolts are determined by calculation. The size and spacing of the reinforcing steel in the concrete wall are determined by calculation. The depth and the width of the wall footing depend on the soil conditions.

Notes · Drawings · Ideas

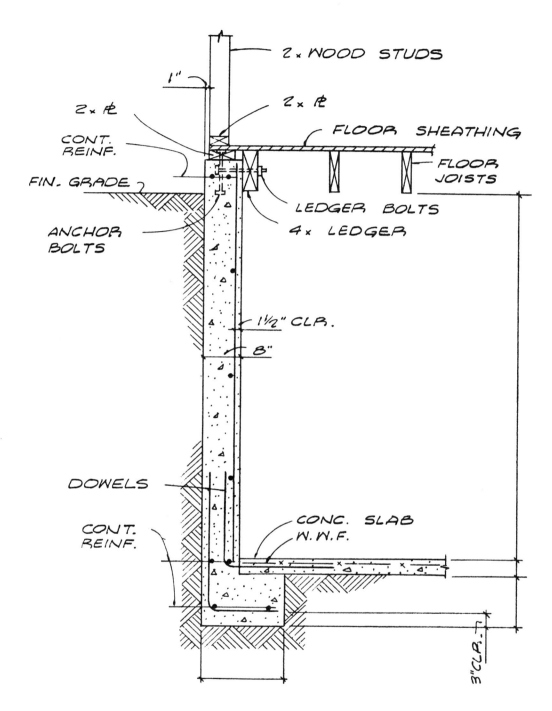

Detail 23(b). A section of a concrete basement wall, wood floor joists and an exterior wood stud wall. The stud wall is set back to allow the exterior wall covering to meet the face of the concrete. The floor joists span parallel to the wall. The floor sheathing is nailed to a 4″ wide wood ledger which is bolted to the concrete wall. The size and spacing of the ledger bolts and the size and spacing of the reinforcing steel in the concrete wall are determined by calculation. The depth and the width of the wall footing depend on soil conditions.

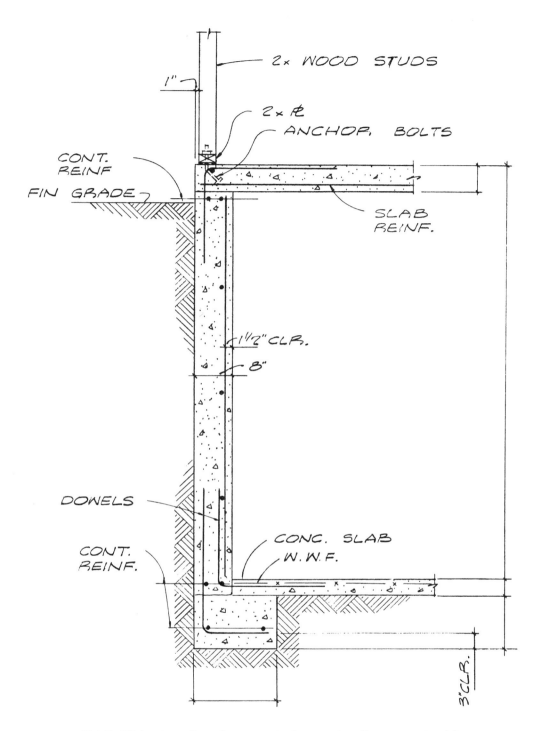

Detail 24(a). A section of a concrete basement wall, a concrete slab, and an exterior wood stud wall. The stud wall is set back to allow the exterior wall covering to meet the face of the concrete. The slab is connected to the wall with reinforcing dowels. The size and spacing of the reinforcing steel in the wall are determined by calculation. The depth and the width of the wall footing depend on the soil conditions.

Notes ▪ Drawings ▪ Ideas

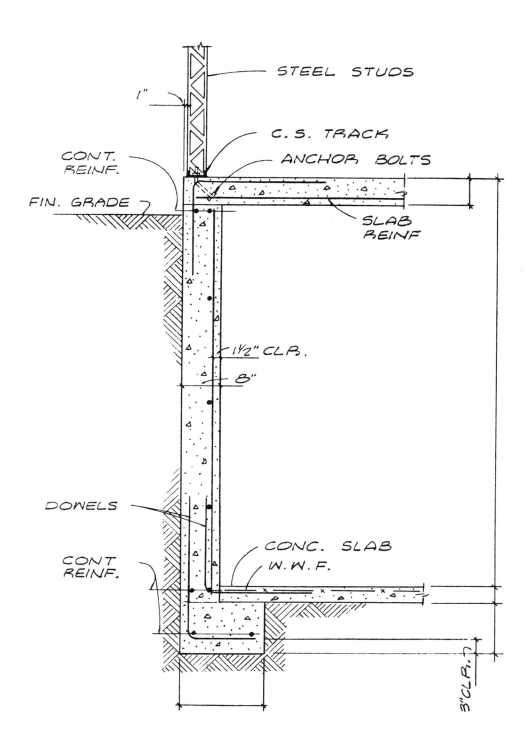

STEEL STUDS

1"

C. S. TRACK

CONT. REINF.

ANCHOR BOLTS

FIN. GRADE

SLAB REINF

1½" CLR.

8"

DOWELS

CONC. SLAB
W. W. F.

CONT REINF.

3"CLR.

Detail 24(b). A section of a concrete basement wall, a concrete slab, and an exterior steel stud wall. The stud wall is set back to allow the exterior wall covering to meet the face of the concrete. The slab is connected to the wall with reinforcing dowels. The size and spacing of the reinforcing steel in the wall are determined by calculation. The depth and the width of the wall footing depend on the soil conditions.

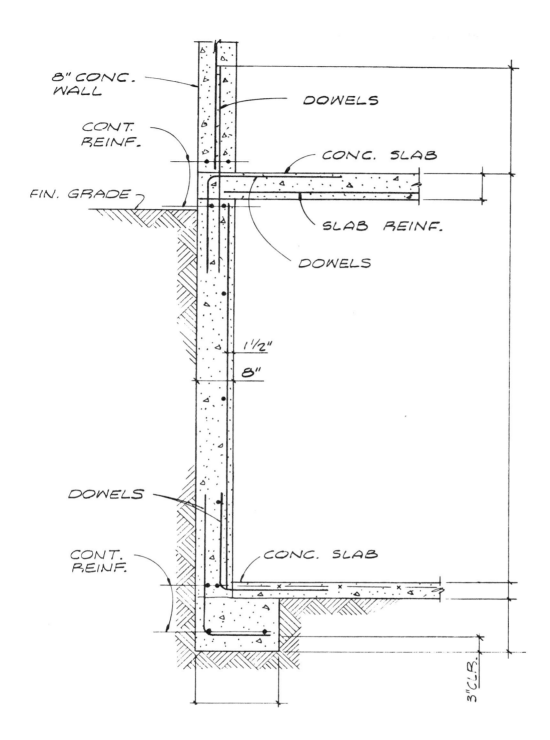

Detail 24(c). A section of a concrete basement wall supporting a concrete slab and a concrete wall. The slab and wall above grade are connected to the basement wall with reinforcing dowels lapped 40 bar diameters or not less than 24″. The size and spacing of the reinforcing steel in the wall are determined by calculation. The depth and the width of the wall footing depend on the soil conditions.

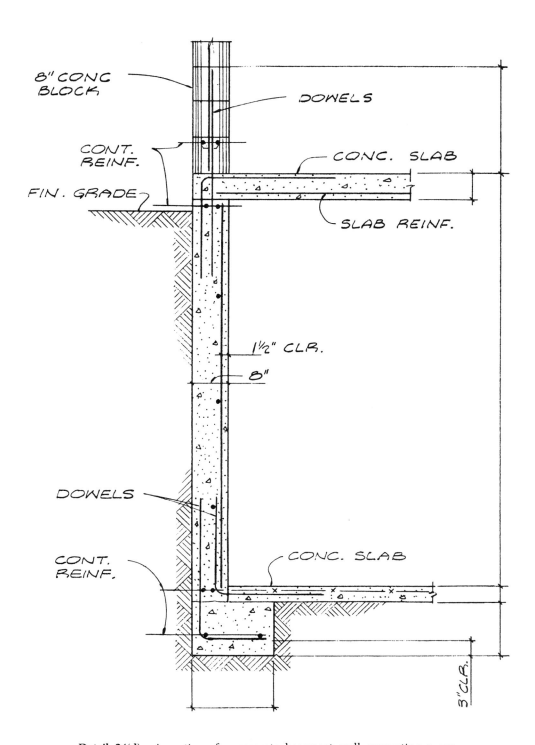

8" CONC BLOCK

DOWELS

CONT. REINF.

CONC. SLAB

FIN. GRADE

SLAB REINF.

1½" CLR.

8"

DOWELS

CONC. SLAB

CONT. REINF.

3" CLR.

Detail 24(d). A section of a concrete basement wall supporting a concrete slab and a concrete block masonry wall. The concrete slab and the masonry wall are connected to the basement wall with reinforcing dowels. The reinforcing dowels lap 40 bar diameters into the concrete and 30 bar diameters into the masonry or not less than 24". The size and spacing of the reinforcing steel in the wall are determined by calculation. The depth and the width of the wall footing depend on the soil conditions.

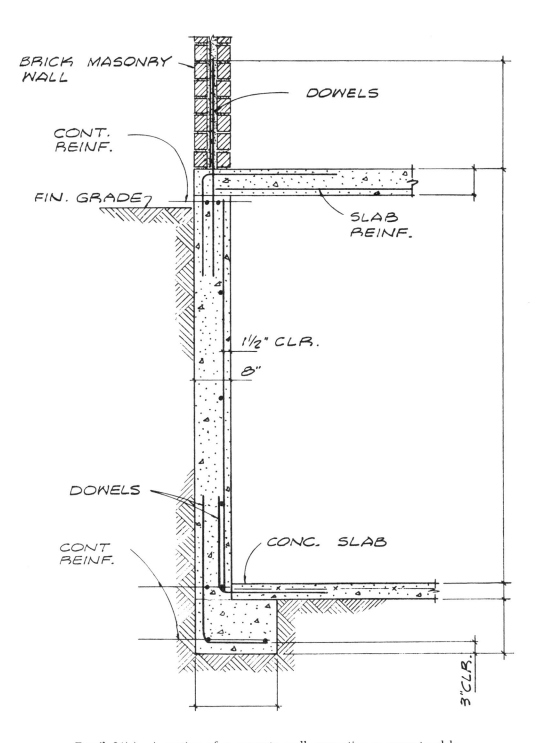

BRICK MASONRY WALL

DOWELS

CONT. REINF.

FIN. GRADE

SLAB REINF.

1½" CLR.

8"

DOWELS

CONT REINF.

CONC. SLAB

3" CLR.

Detail 24(e). A section of a concrete wall supporting a concrete slab and a brick wall. The concrete slab and the brick wall are connected to the basement wall with reinforcing dowels. The reinforcing dowels lap 40 bar diameters into the concrete and 30 bar diameters into the masonry or not less than 24″. The size and spacing of the reinforcing steel in the wall are determined by calculation. The depth and the width of the wall footing depend on the soil conditions.

Notes ▪ Drawings ▪ Ideas

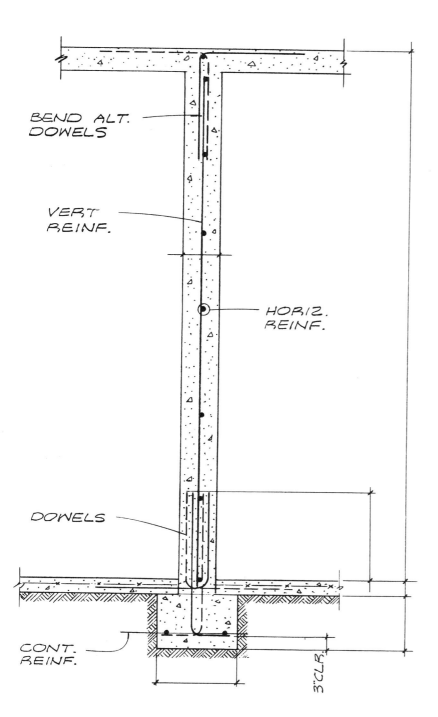

BEND ALT.
DOWELS

VERT
REINF.

HORIZ.
REINF.

DOWELS

CONT.
REINF.

3"CLR.

Detail 25. A section of a one story interior concrete wall supporting a concrete slab. The wall is connected to the slab at the top of the wall and to the footing at the bottom of the wall with reinforcing dowels bent in alternate directions. The size and spacing of the wall reinforcement are determined by calculation. Concrete walls greater than 8″ thick require reinforcement on each face. The depth and the width of the wall footing depend on the soil conditions.

Notes ▪ Drawings ▪ Ideas

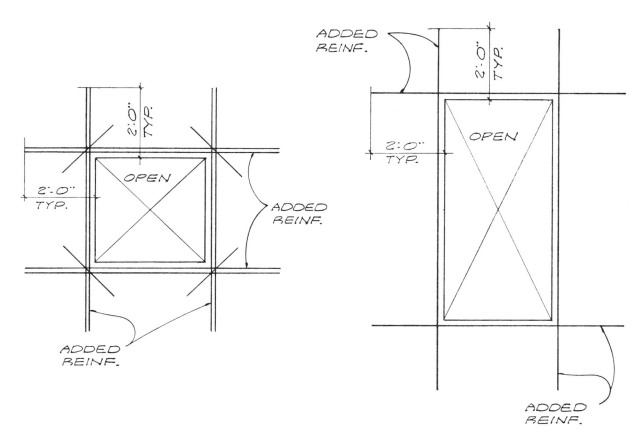

Detail 26(a). Elevations of openings in concrete walls. Additional reinforcing steel is placed at the edges of the wall opening. The added vertical and horizontal bars extend a minimum of 24″ past the edge of the opening. The diagonal bars at the corners are optional.

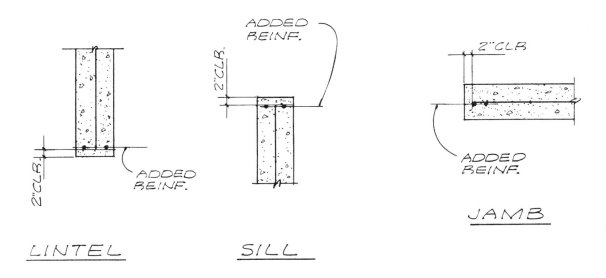

LINTEL

SILL

JAMB

Detail 26(b). Sections of a concrete wall opening, lintel, jamb, and sill. The sill and jamb edges are nominally reinforced with two bars. The lintel may require more than two reinforcing bars depending on the span of the opening and the load to be supported.

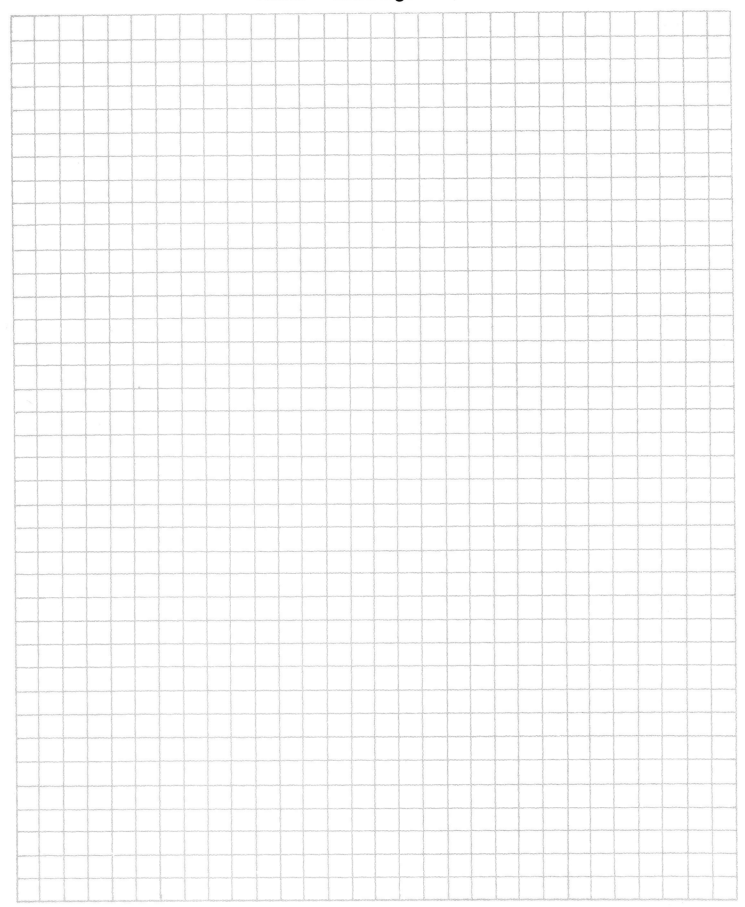

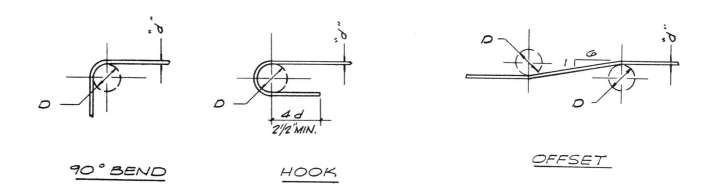

90° BEND   HOOK   OFFSET

TYPICAL REINF. BAR BENDS

D = BAR DIAM;
d = BEND DIAM.
MIN D = 6d FOR #7 BARS OR SMALLER
     D = 8d FOR #8 BARS OR LARGER
     D = 5d FOR STIRRUPS AND TIES

Detail 27(a). Details of reinforcing bar standard bends and hooks.

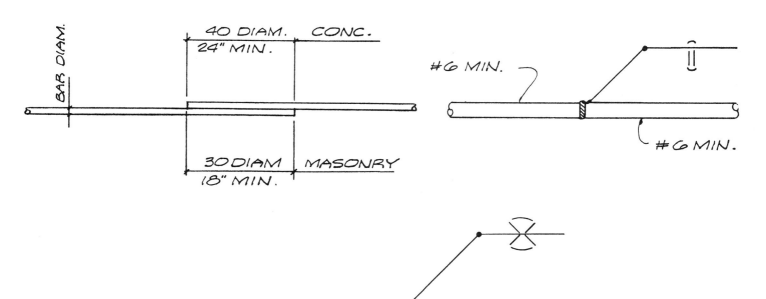

Detail 27(b). Details of reinforcing bar lap splices and welded splices.

71

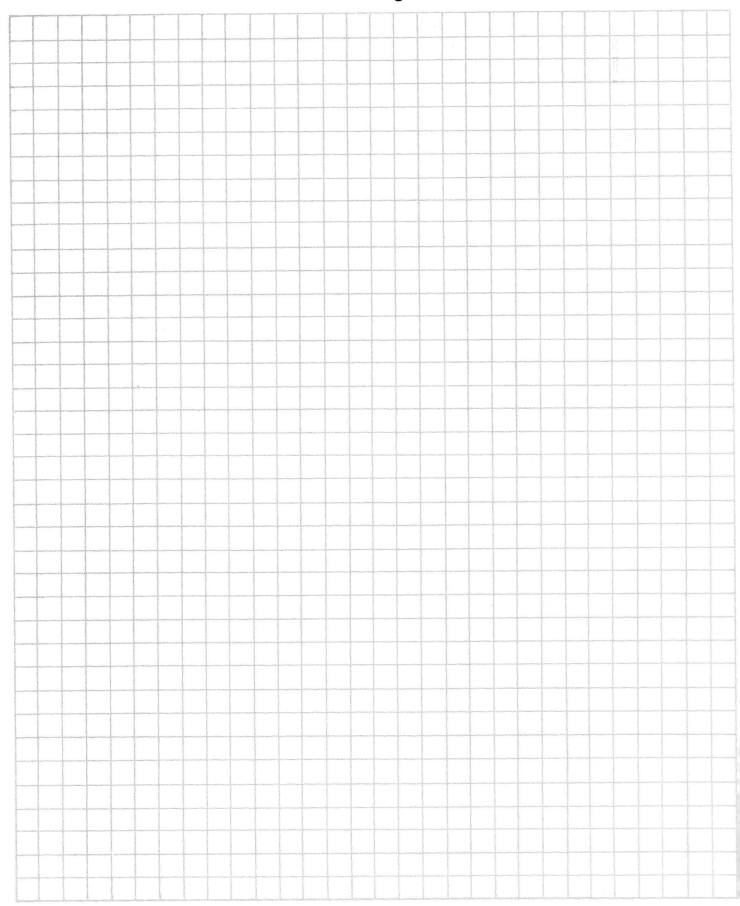

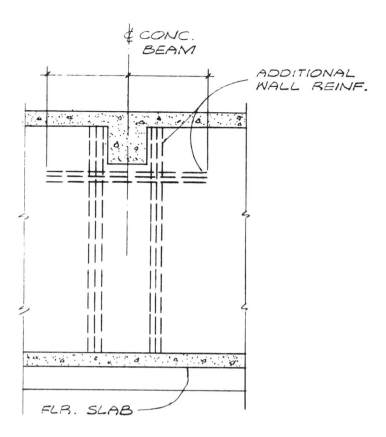

Detail 28. A section of a concrete beam supported by a concrete wall. The beam reaction on the wall is supported by added reinforcement in the wall as shown. The size and spacing of the added reinforcement are determined by calculation.

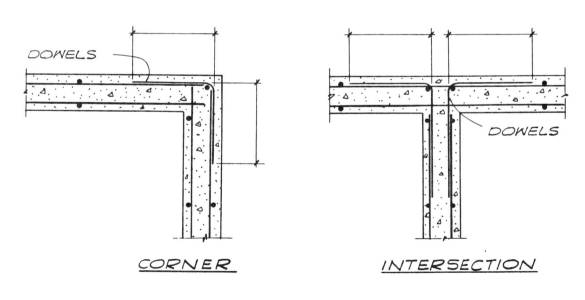

CORNER   INTERSECTION

Detail 29(a). A plan section of the reinforcing steel intersection of concrete wall bond beams. The reinforcing bars are lapped 40 bar diameters or not less than 24″.

Detail 29(b). A plan section of the reinforcing steel at the corner of a concrete wall bond beam. The bond beams are connected by reinforcing dowels of the same size as the bond beam reinforcing bars. The length of the lap splice is 40 bar diameters or not less than 24″.

Notes ▪ Drawings ▪ Ideas

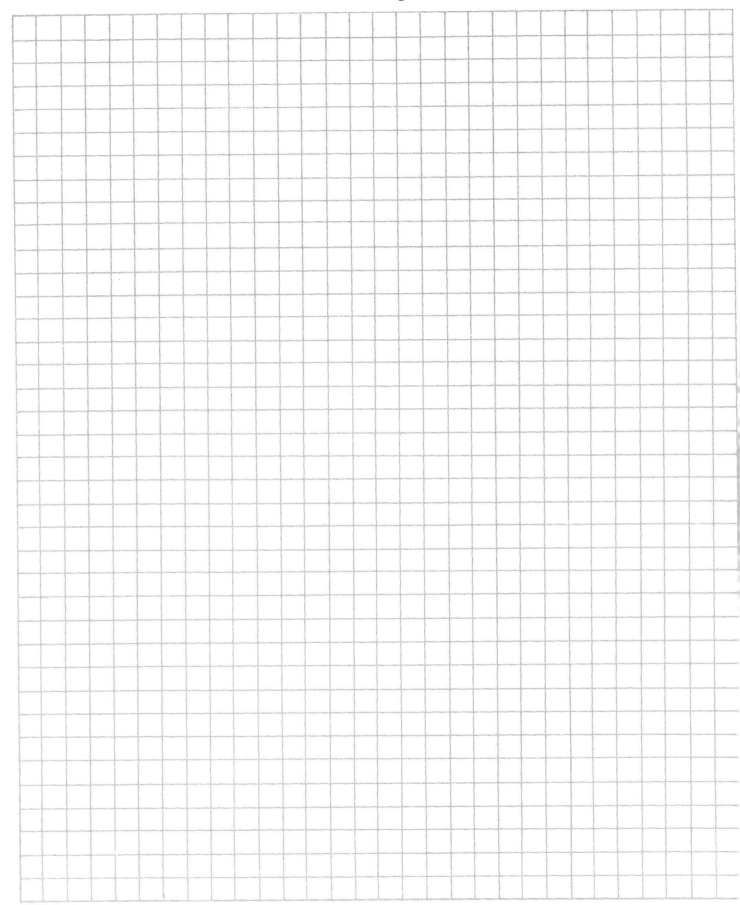

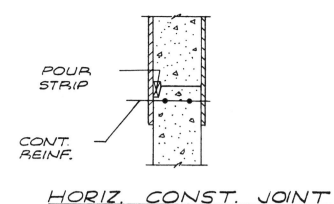

POUR STRIP

CONT. REINF.

HORIZ. CONST. JOINT

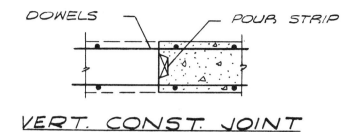

DOWELS

POUR STRIP

VERT. CONST. JOINT

Detail 30(a). Sections of concrete wall construction joints. The location of a concrete construction joint for thermal expansion and contraction or because of a concrete pour stop is determined by the engineer. All surface laitance must be removed from the previous pour before a new concrete pour is made. It may be necessary to waterproof a concrete wall construction joint, depending on the conditions of use of the wall. Construction joints in concrete walls should not be made at points of high bending or high shear unless specifically provided for in the design of the wall.

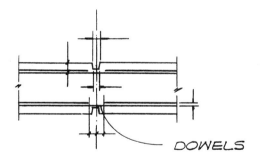

DOWELS

TYP. CONTROL JT.

Detail 30(b). A section of a vertical control joint in a concrete wall. The location of the wall control joint is determined by the engineer. Control joints should not be located at points of high bending or shear unless specifically provided for in the design of the wall.

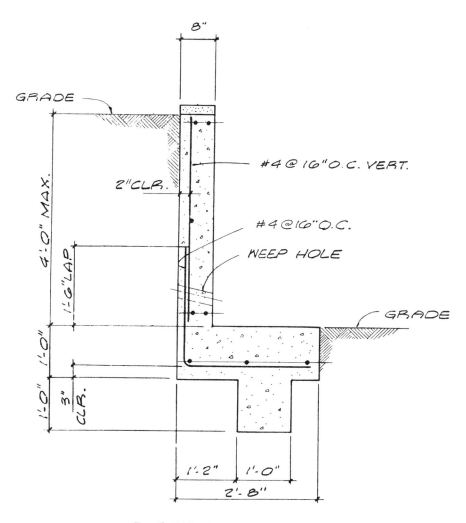

Detail 31(a). Stem height 4′0″.

Detail 31. Sections of concrete retaining walls with soil at the exterior face of the stem. The wall retains a flat grade with no surcharge. The wall dimensions and reinforcing steel size and spacing are determined by calculation. Two #4 horizontal continuous reinforcing bars are placed at the top and at the bottom of the wall stem. The minimum horizontal reinforcement in the stem wall and the footing is #4 at 24″ o.c. A 3″ dia. galvanized iron pipe space at 8′0″ o.c. is placed at the base of the stem to act as a weep hole. The cement cap at the top of the wall is optional. The walls are designed for 30 lb per cu ft equivalent fluid pressure and a maximum soil pressure of 1500 lb per sq ft. The resultant of the forces passes through the middle ⅓ of the wall footing. The walls are designed to resist sliding and overturning. The overturning safety factor is 1.5. The concrete design stress is $f'c = 2000$ psi.

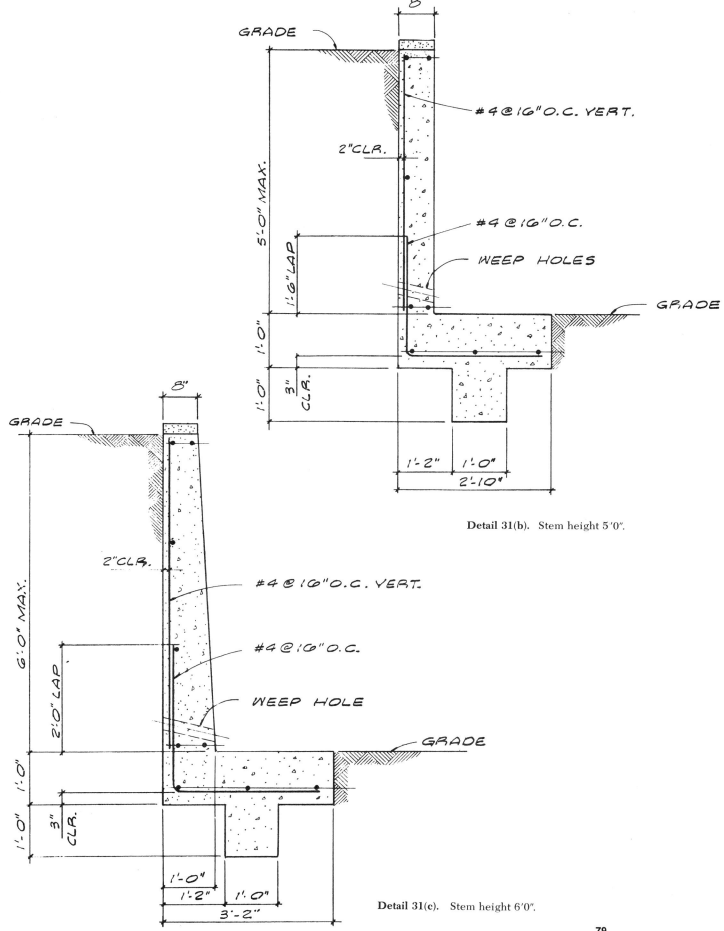

GRADE

8"

#4@16"O.C. VERT.

2"CLR.

5'-0" MAX.

1'-6"LAP

#4@16"O.C.

WEEP HOLES

GRADE

1'-0"

1'-0"

3" CLR.

1'-2"   1'-0"

2'-10"

Detail 31(b). Stem height 5′0″.

GRADE

8"

2"CLR.

#4@16"O.C. VERT.

6'-0" MAX.

2'-0"LAP

#4@16"O.C.

WEEP HOLE

GRADE

1'-0"

1'-0"

3" CLR.

1'-0"

1'-2"   1'-0"

3'-2"

Detail 31(c). Stem height 6′0″.

79

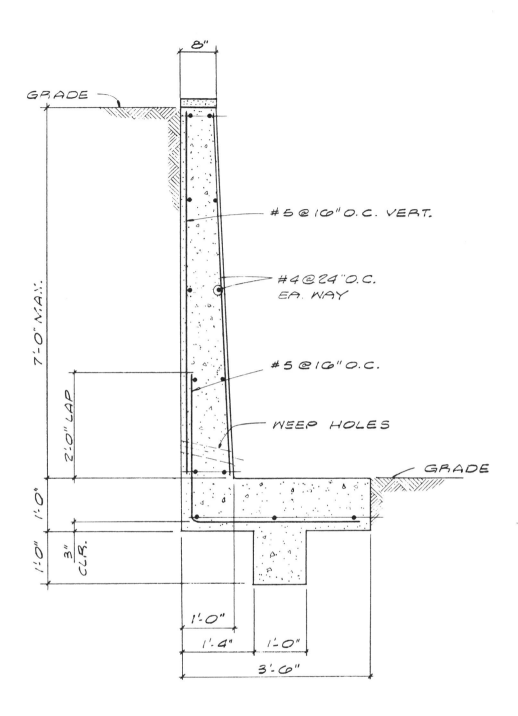

8"

GRADE

#5 @ 16" O.C. VERT.

#4 @ 24" O.C. EA. WAY

7'-0" MAX.

#5 @ 16" O.C.

2'-0" LAP

WEEP HOLES

GRADE

1'-0"

1'-0"

3" CLR.

1'-0"

1'-4"   1'-0"

3'-6"

Detail 31(d).   Stem height 7′0″.

Notes ▪ Drawings ▪ Ideas

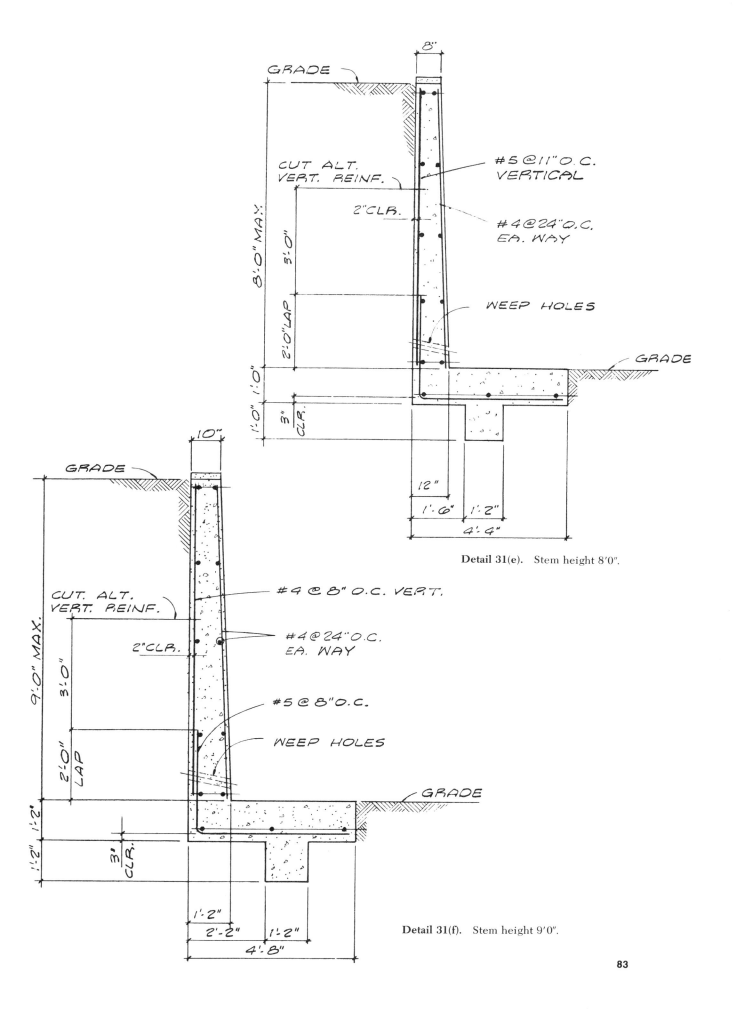

GRADE

8"

CUT ALT.
VERT. REINF.

#5 @11" O.C.
VERTICAL

2"CLR.

#4 @24" O.C.
EA. WAY

8'-0" MAX.

3'-0"

2'-0"LAP

WEEP HOLES

GRADE

1'-0" 1'-0"

3"
CLR.

12"

1'-6" 1'-2"

4'-4"

Detail 31(e). Stem height 8'0".

GRADE

10"

CUT. ALT.
VERT. REINF.

#4 @ 8" O.C. VERT.

2"CLR.

#4 @24" O.C.
EA. WAY

9'-0" MAX.

3'-0"

2'-0"
LAP

#5 @ 8" O.C.

WEEP HOLES

GRADE

1'-2" 1'-2"

3'
CLR.

1'-2"

2'-2" 1'-2"

4'-8"

Detail 31(f). Stem height 9'0".

83

Notes ▪ Drawings ▪ Ideas

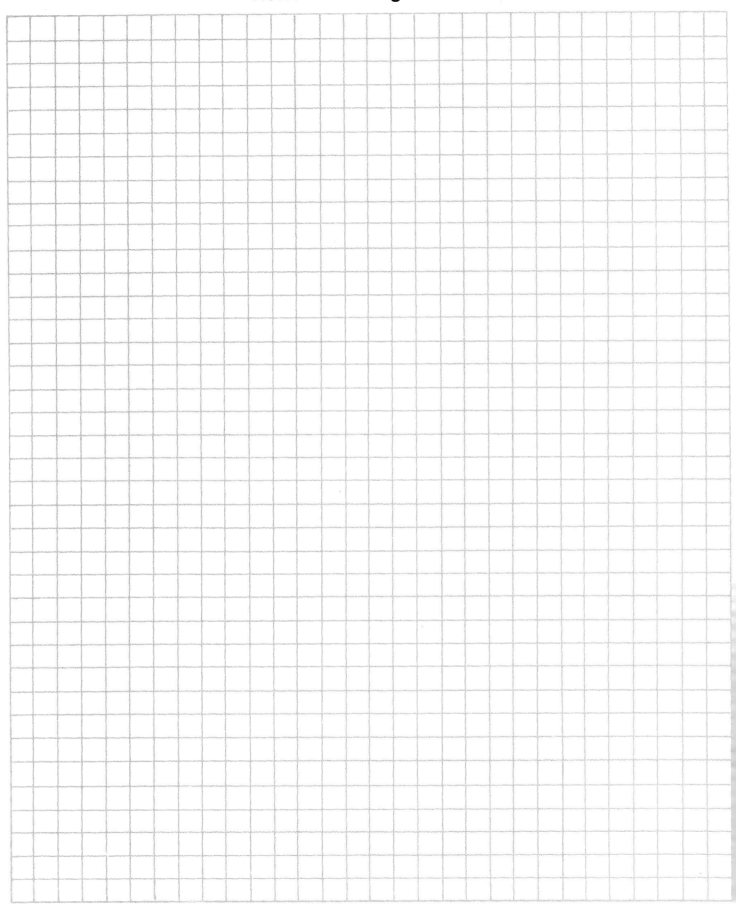

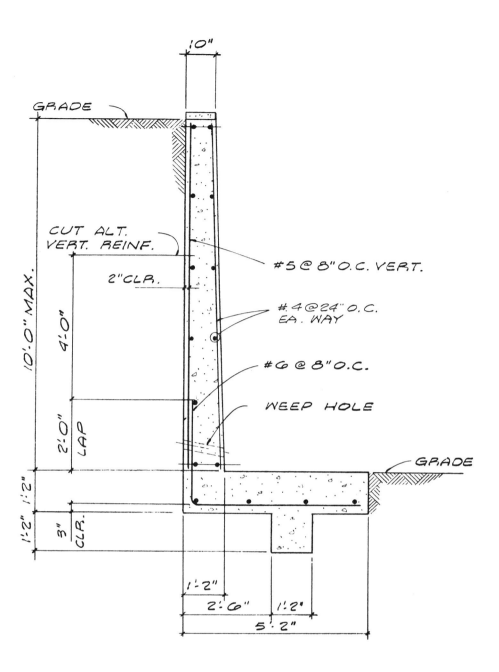

GRADE

10"

CUT ALT.
VERT. REINF.

2" CLR.

10'-0" MAX.

4'-0"

2'-0" LAP

1'-2" 1'-2"

3" CLR.

#5 @ 8" O.C. VERT.

#4 @ 24" O.C.
EA. WAY

#6 @ 8" O.C.

WEEP HOLE

GRADE

1'-2"

2'-6"   1'-2"

5'-2"

Detail 31(g).   Stem height 10'0".

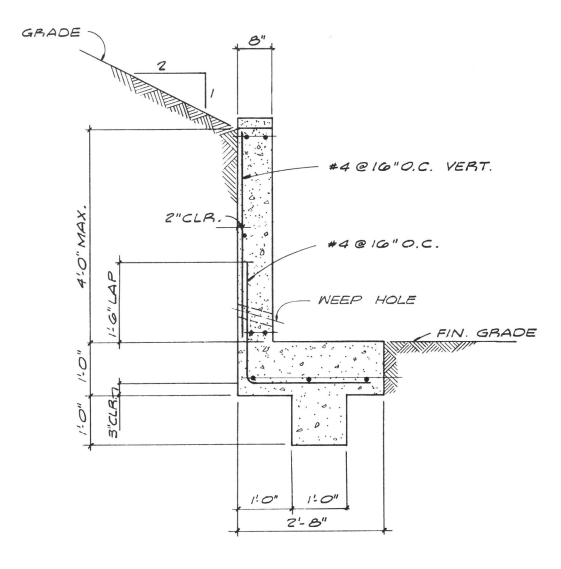

GRADE

8"

2
1

#4 @ 16" O.C. VERT.

2" CLR.

4'-0" MAX.

1'-6" LAP

#4 @ 16" O.C.

WEEP HOLE

FIN. GRADE

1'-0"

1'-0"

3" CLR.

1'-0"   1'-0"

2'-8"

Detail 32(a). Stem height 4'0".

Detail 32. Sections of concrete retaining walls with soil at the exterior face of the stem. The walls retain a grade slope of two horizontal to one vertical and no surcharge. The wall dimensions and reinforcing steel size and spacing are determined by calculation. Two #4 horizontal continuous reinforcing bars are placed at the top and the bottom of the wall stem. The minimum horizontal reinforcement in the stem wall and the footing is #4 at 24" o.c. A 3" dia. galvanized iron pipe spaced at 8'0" o.c. is placed at the base of the stem to act as a weep hole. The cement cap at the top of the wall is optional. The walls are designed for 43 lb per cu ft equivalent fluid pressure and a maximum soil pressure of 1500 lb per sq ft. The resultant of the forces passes through the middle $\frac{1}{3}$ of the wall footing. The walls are designed to resist sliding and overturning. The overturning safety factor is 1.5. The concrete design stress is $f'c = 2000$ psi.

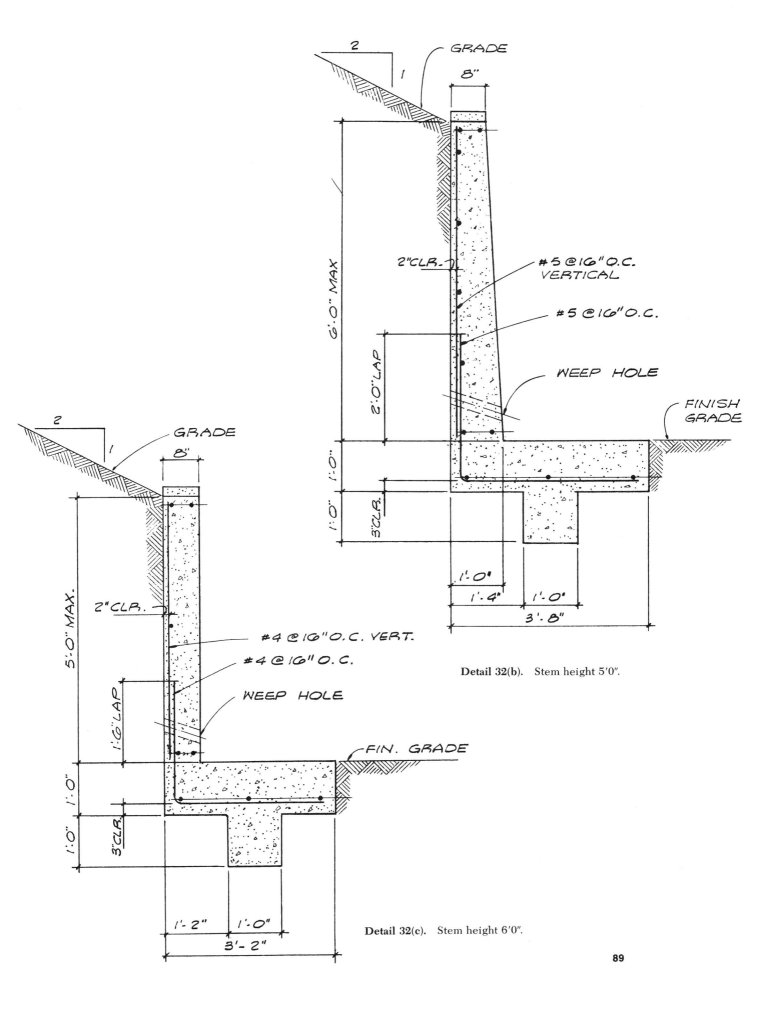

GRADE

2
1

8"

6'-0" MAX

2" CLR.

#5 @ 16" O.C.
VERTICAL

#5 @ 16" O.C.

WEEP HOLE

2'-0" LAP

FINISH
GRADE

1'-0"

1'-0"

3" CLR.

1'-0"

1'-4"   1'-0"

3'-8"

Detail 32(b). Stem height 5'0".

GRADE

2
1

8"

5'-0" MAX.

2" CLR.

#4 @ 16" O.C. VERT.

#4 @ 16" O.C.

WEEP HOLE

1'-6" LAP

FIN. GRADE

1'-0"

1'-0"

3" CLR.

1'-2"   1'-0"

3'-2"

Detail 32(c). Stem height 6'0".

89

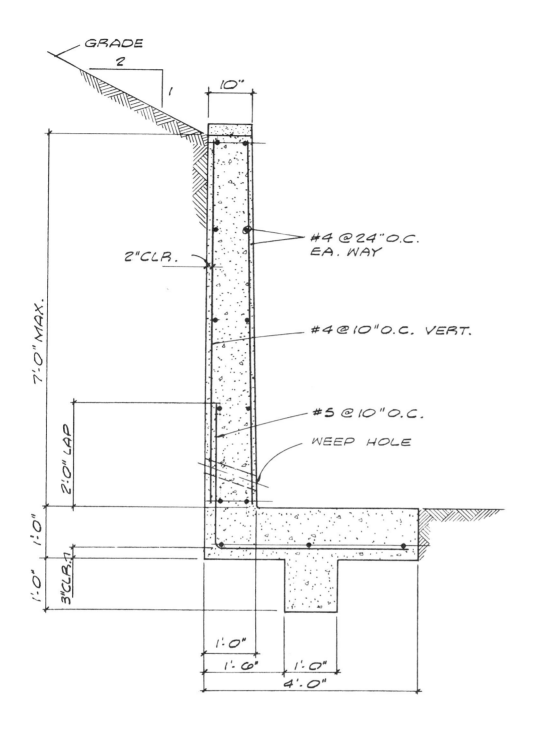

GRADE
2
1

10"

#4 @24"O.C.
EA. WAY

2"CLR.

#4 @10"O.C. VERT.

7'-0"MAX.

2'-0" LAP

#5 @10"O.C.

WEEP HOLE

1'-0"

1'-0"

3"CLR.

1'-0"

1'-6"

1'-0"

4'-0"

Detail 32(d). Stem height 7'0".

Notes ▪ Drawings ▪ Ideas

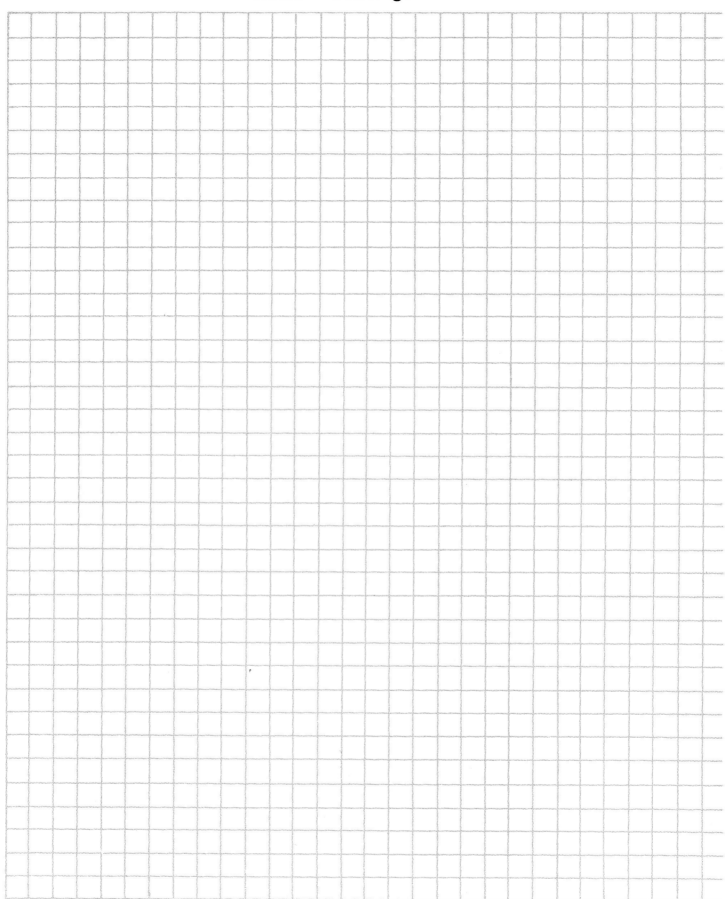

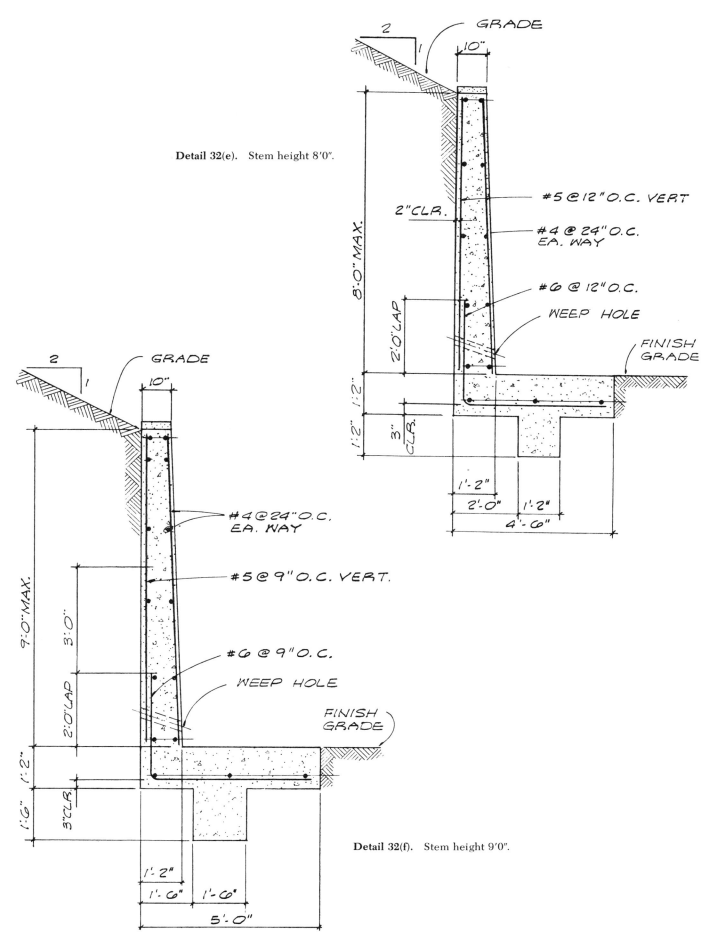

Detail 32(e). Stem height 8′0″.

GRADE

2

1

10″

8′-0″ MAX.

2″ CLR.

#5 @ 12″ O.C. VERT

#4 @ 24″ O.C.
EA. WAY

#6 @ 12″ O.C.

WEEP HOLE

FINISH GRADE

2′-0″ LAP

1′-2″

1′-2″

3″ CLR.

1′-2″

2′-0″

1′-2″

4′-6″

GRADE

2

1

10″

9′-0″ MAX.

3′-0″

2′-0″ LAP

1′-6″

1′-2″

3″ CLR.

#4 @ 24″ O.C.
EA. WAY

#5 @ 9″ O.C. VERT.

#6 @ 9″ O.C.

WEEP HOLE

FINISH GRADE

1′-2″

1′-6″

1′-6″

5′-0″

Detail 32(f). Stem height 9′0″.

Notes ▪ Drawings ▪ Ideas

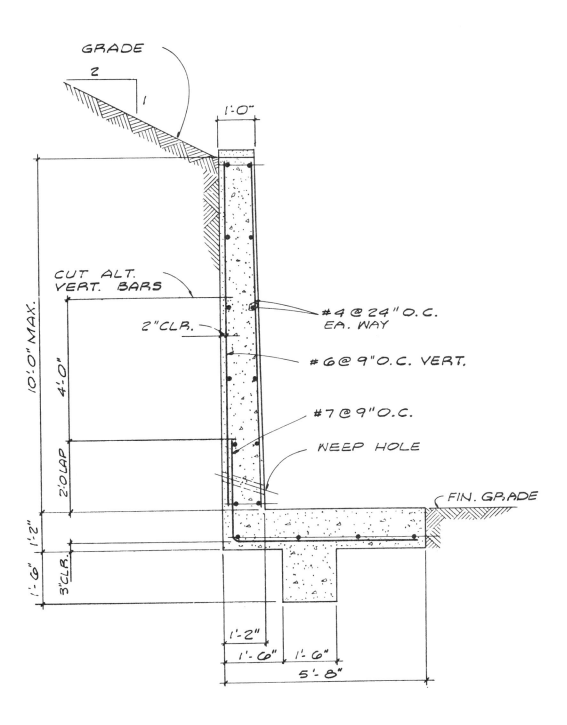

GRADE

2
1

1'-0"

CUT ALT.
VERT. BARS

10'-0" MAX.

4'-0"

2"CLR.

2'-0 LAP

1'-2"

1'-6"

3"CLR.

#4 @ 24" O.C.
EA. WAY

#6 @ 9" O.C. VERT.

#7 @ 9" O.C.

WEEP HOLE

FIN. GRADE

1'-2"
1'-6"   1'-6"
5'-8"

Detail 32(g). Stem height 10'0".

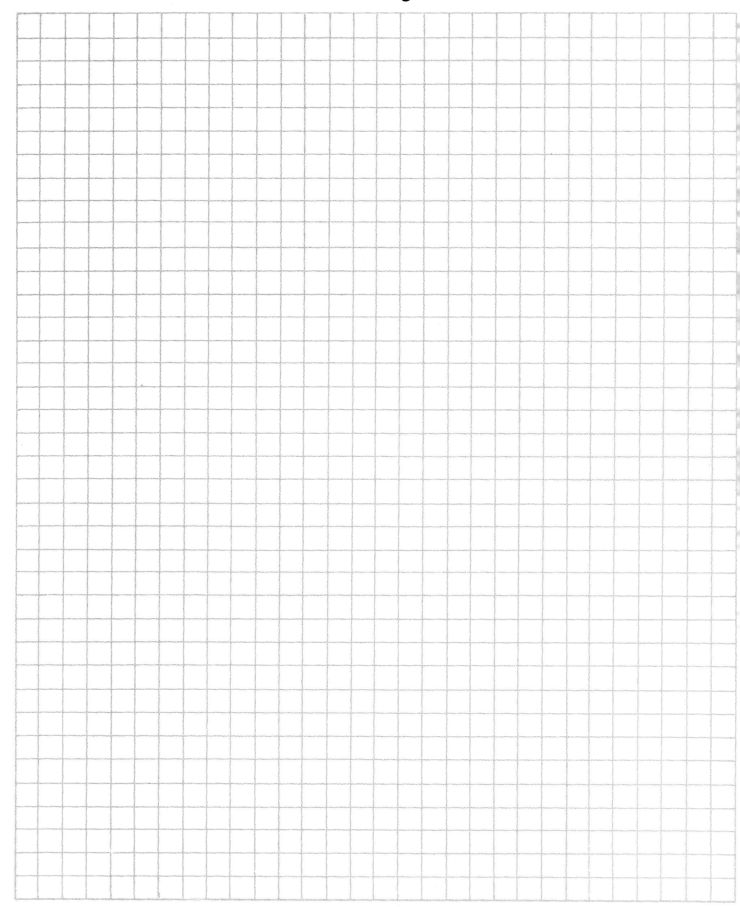

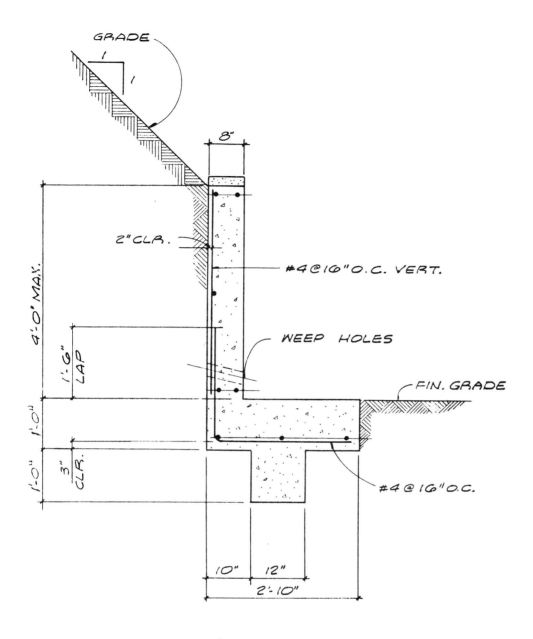

GRADE

8″

2″ CLR.

#4 @ 16″ O.C. VERT.

WEEP HOLES

FIN. GRADE

#4 @ 16″ O.C.

4′-0″ MAX.

1′-6″ LAP

1′-0″

1′-0″

3″ CLR.

10″   12″

2′-10″

Detail 33(a).   Stem height 4′0″.

Detail 33. Sections of concrete retaining walls with soil at the exterior face of the stem. The wall retains a sloping grade with one horizontal to one vertical and no surcharge. The wall dimensions and reinforcing steel size and spacing are determined by calculation. Two #4 horizontal continuous reinforcing bars are placed at the top and the bottom of the wall stem. The minimum horizontal reinforcement in the stem wall and the footing is #4 at 24″ o.c. A 3″ dia. galvanized iron pipe spaced at 8′0″ o.c. is placed at the base of the stem to act as a weep hole. The cement cap at the top of the wall is optional. The walls are designed for 80 lb per cu ft equivalent fluid pressure and a maximum soil pressure of 1500 lb per sq ft. The resultant of forces passes through the middle ⅓ of the wall footing. The walls are designed to resist sliding and overturning. The overturning safety factor is 1.5. The concrete design stress is $f'c = 2000$ psi.

Notes ▪ Drawings ▪ Ideas

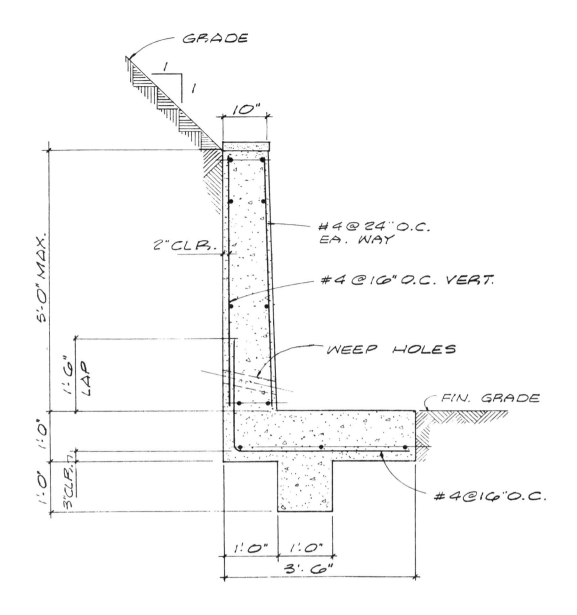

GRADE

10"

5'-0" MAX.

#4 @ 24" O.C.
EA. WAY

2" CLR.

#4 @ 16" O.C. VERT.

1'-6" LAP

WEEP HOLES

FIN. GRADE

1'-0' 1'-0'

3" CLR.

#4 @ 16" O.C.

1'-0" 1'-0"

3'-6"

Detail 33(b). Stem height 5′0″.

Notes ▪ Drawings ▪ Ideas

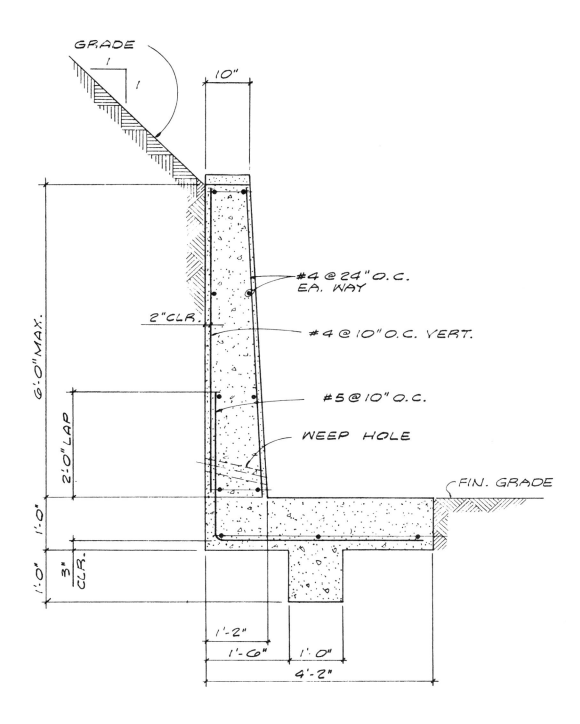

GRADE

10"

#4 @ 24" O.C.
EA. WAY

2" CLR.

#4 @ 10" O.C. VERT.

#5 @ 10" O.C.

WEEP HOLE

FIN. GRADE

6'-0" MAX.

2'-0" LAP

1'-0"

1'-0"

3" CLR.

1'-2"

1'-6"

1'-0"

4'-2"

Detail 33(c). Stem height 6'0".

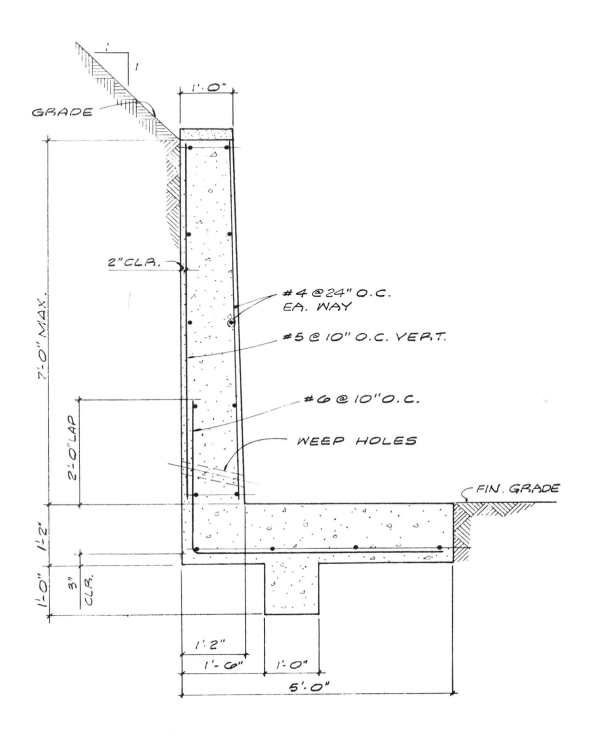

GRADE

1'-0"

7'-0" MAX.

2" CLR.

#4 @ 24" O.C.
EA. WAY

#5 @ 10" O.C. VERT.

#6 @ 10" O.C.

WEEP HOLES

2'-0" LAP

1'-2"

3" CLR.

1'-0"

FIN. GRADE

1'-2"

1'-6"   1'-0"

5'-0"

Detail 33(d). Stem height 7'0".

Notes ▪ Drawings ▪ Ideas

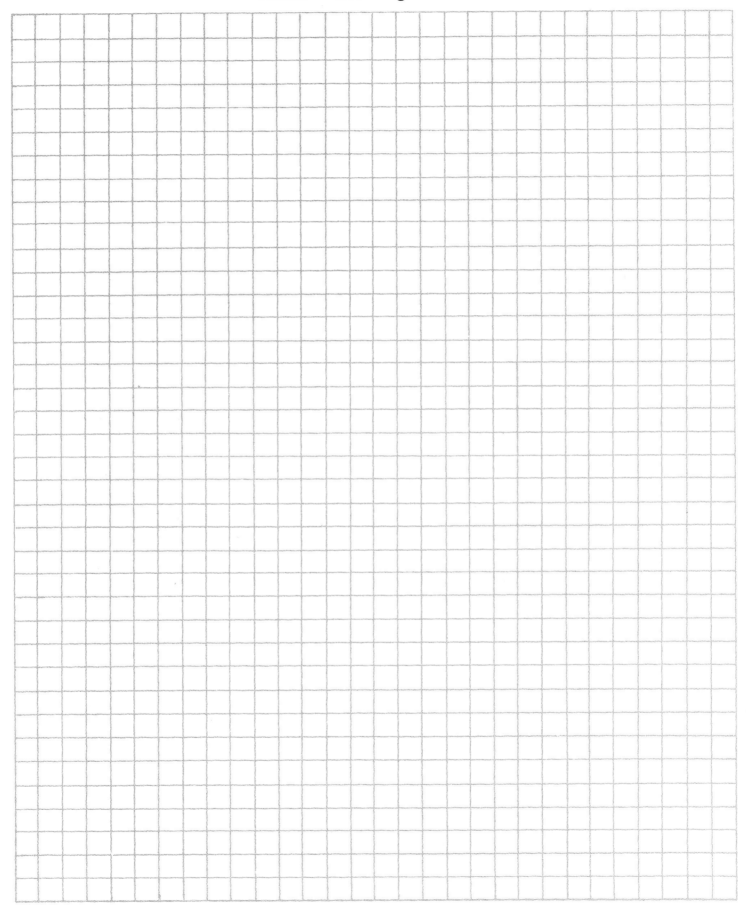

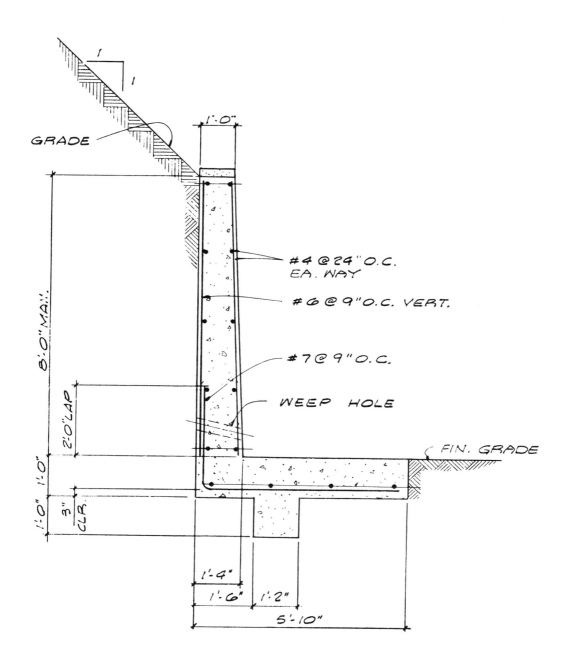

GRADE

1'-0"

#4 @ 24" O.C.
EA. WAY

#6 @ 9" O.C. VERT.

#7 @ 9" O.C.

WEEP HOLE

FIN. GRADE

8'-0" MAX.

2'-0" LAP

1'-0"

1'-0"

3" CLR.

1'-4"

1'-6" 1'-2"

5'-10"

Detail 33(e).   Stem height 8′0″.

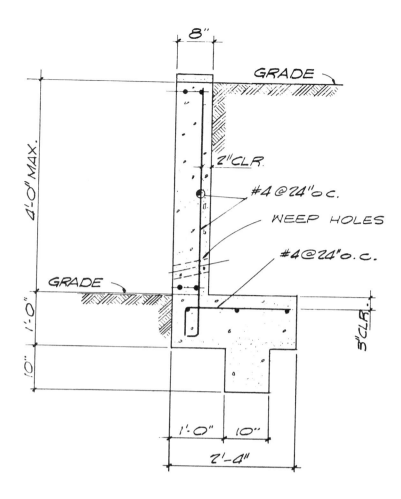

Detail 34(a). Stem height 40″.

Detail 34. Sections of concrete retaining walls with soil at the interior face of the stem. The walls retain a flat grade with no surcharge. The wall dimensions and reinforcing steel size and spacing are determined by calculation. Two #4 horizontal continuous reinforcing bars are placed at the top and the bottom of the wall stem. The minimum horizontal reinforcement in the stem wall and the footing is #4 at 24″ o.c. A 3″ dia. galvanized iron pipe spaced at 8′0″ o.c. is placed at the base of the stem to act as a weep hole. The cement cap at the top of the wall is optional. The walls are designed for a 30 lb per cu ft equivalent fluid pressure and a maximum soil pressure of 1500 lb per sq ft. The resultant of the forces passes through the middle ⅓ of the wall footing. The walls are designed to resist sliding and overturning. The overturning safety factor is 1.5. The concrete design stress is $f'c = 2000$ psi.

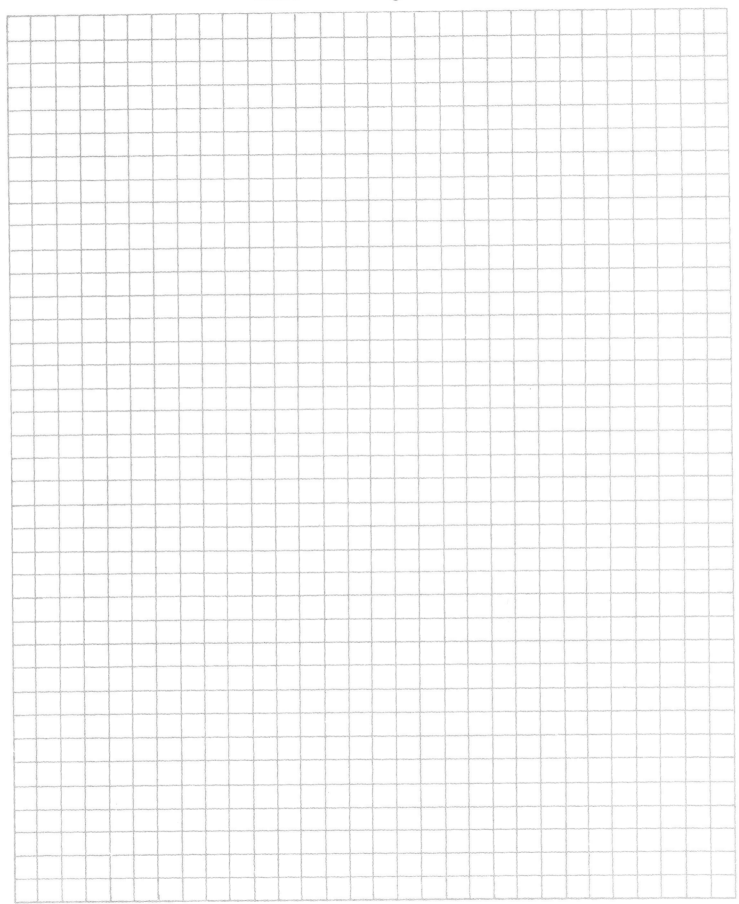

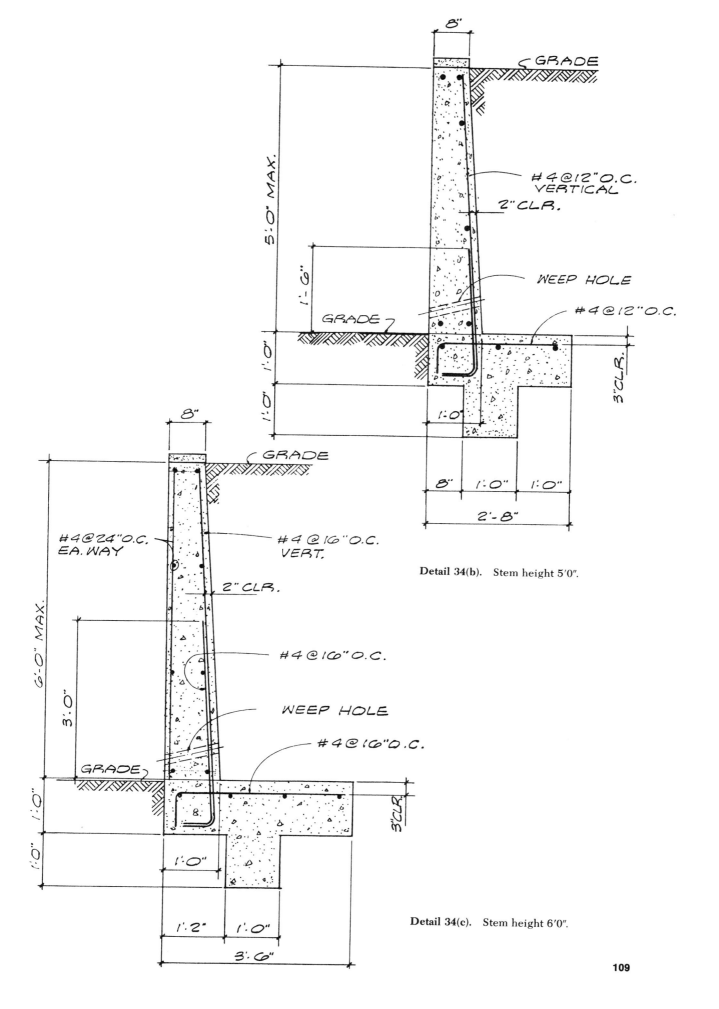

8"

GRADE

#4@12"O.C.
VERTICAL

2" CLR.

5'0" MAX.

1'-6"

GRADE

WEEP HOLE

#4@12"O.C.

1'0"

3" CLR.

1'0"

1'0"

8"   1'0"   1'0"

2'-8"

Detail 34(b).   Stem height 5'0".

8"

GRADE

#4@24"O.C.
EA. WAY

#4@16"O.C.
VERT.

2" CLR.

#4@16"O.C.

WEEP HOLE

6'0" MAX.

3'0"

#4@16"O.C.

GRADE

3" CLR.

1'0"

1'0"

8"

1'2"   1'0"

3'6"

Detail 34(c).   Stem height 6'0".

Notes · Drawings · Ideas

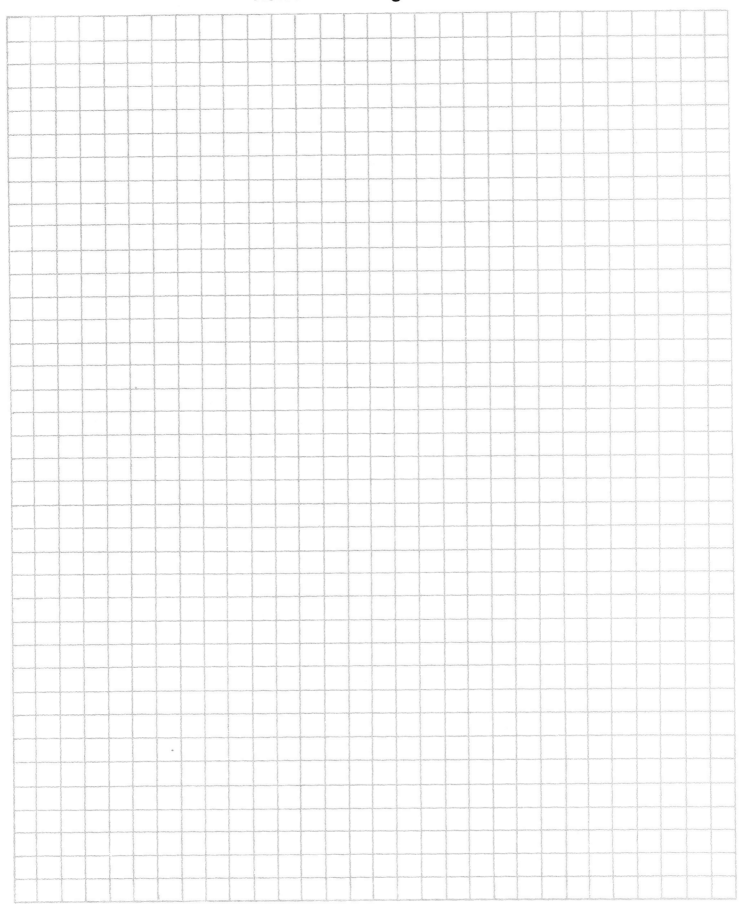

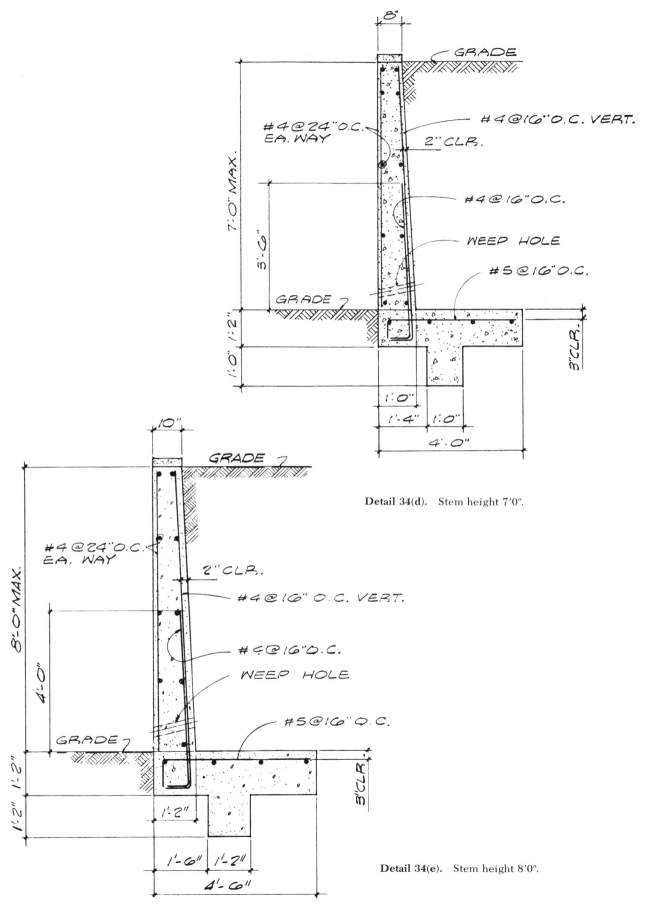

Detail 34(d). Stem height 7′0″.

Detail 34(e). Stem height 8′0″.

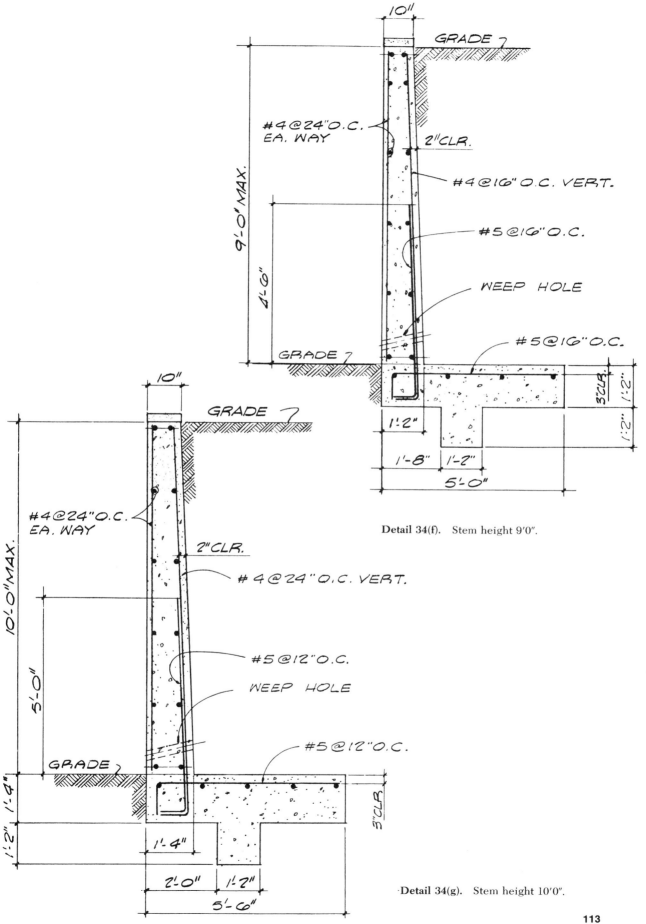

Detail 34(f). Stem height 9′0″.

Detail 34(g). Stem height 10′0″.

113

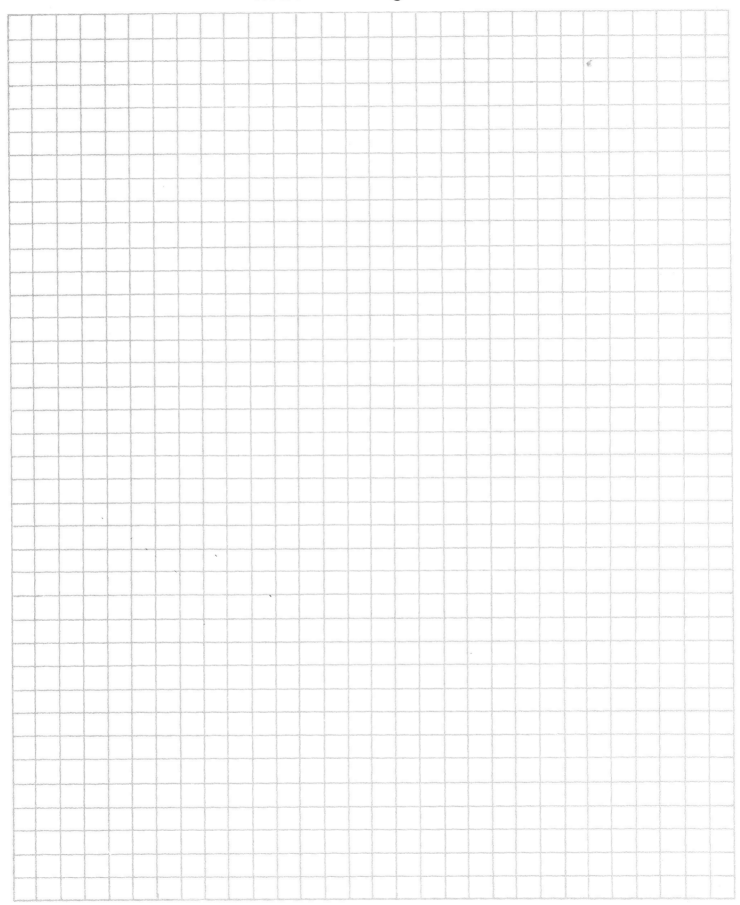

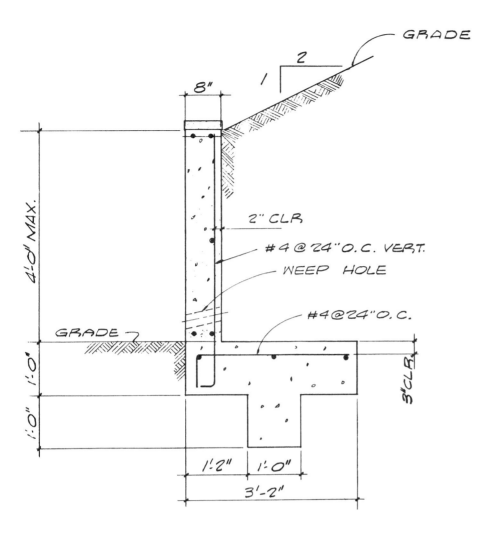

Detail 35(a).   Stem height 4′0″.

Detail 35. Sections of concrete retaining walls with soil at the interior face of the stem. The wall retains a sloping grade of two horizontal to one vertical and no surcharge. The wall dimensions and reinforcing steel size and spacing are determined by calculation. Two #4 horizontal continuous reinforcing bars are placed at the top and the bottom of the stem. The minimum horizontal reinforcement in the stem wall and the footing is #4 at 24″ o.c. A 3″ dia. galvanized iron pipe spaced at 8′0″ o.c. is placed at the base of the stem to act as a weep hole. The cement cap at the top of the wall is optional. The walls are designed for 43 lb per cu ft equivalent fluid pressure and a maximum soil pressure of 1500 lb per sq ft. The resultant of the forces passes through the middle ⅓ of the wall footing. The walls are designed to resist sliding and overturning. The overturning safety factor is 1.5. The concrete design stress is $f'c = 2000$ psi.

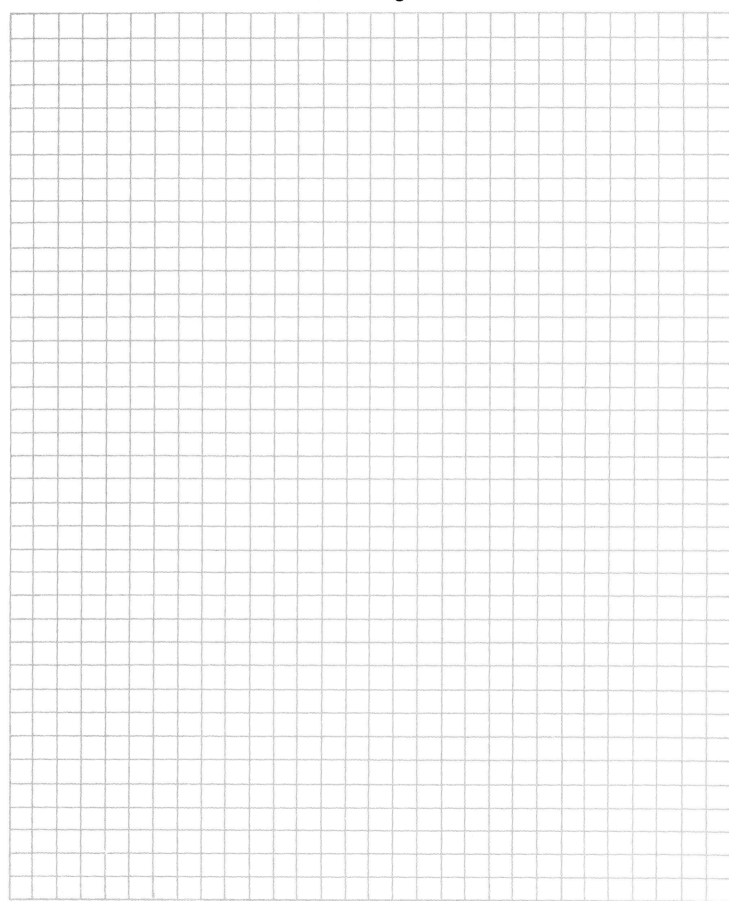

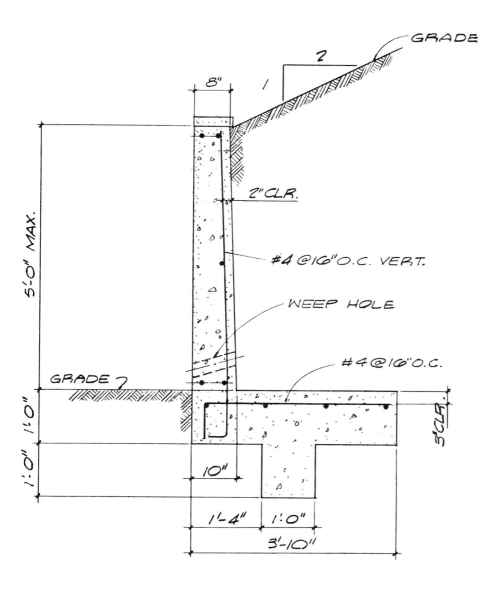

GRADE

2

1

8"

2" CLR.

#4 @ 16" O.C. VERT.

WEEP HOLE

#4 @ 16" O.C.

3" CLR.

GRADE

5'-0" MAX.

1'-0"

1'-0"

10"

1'-4"

1'-0"

3'-10"

Detail 35(b).   Stem height 5'0".

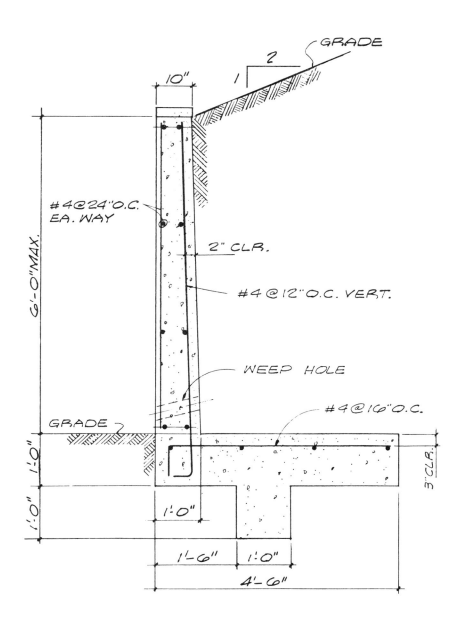

Detail 35(c). Stem height 6'0".

Notes · Drawings · Ideas

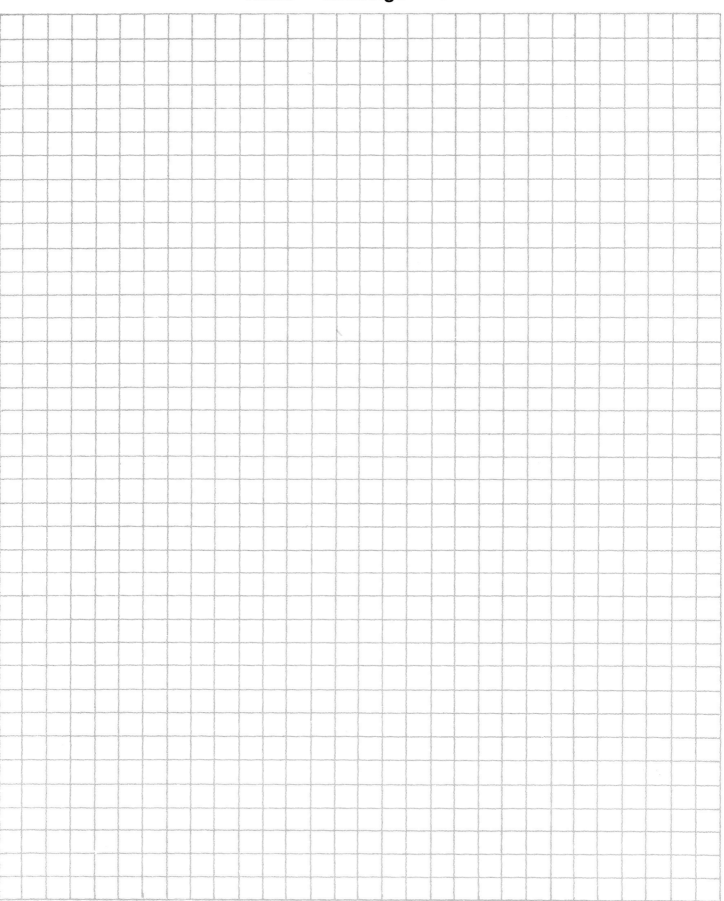

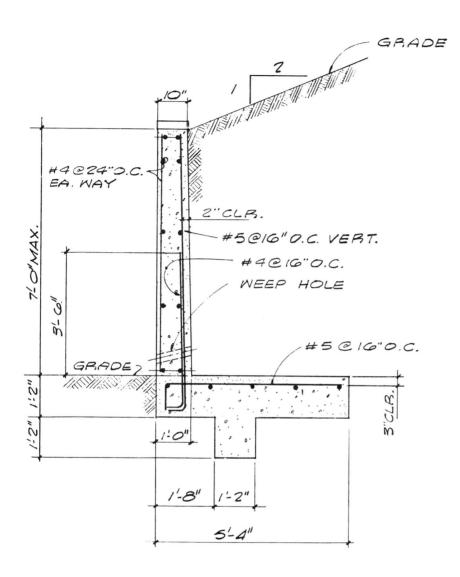

GRADE

2

1

10"

#4@24"O.C.
EA. WAY

2" CLR.

#5@16" O.C. VERT.

#4@16" O.C.

WEEP HOLE

#5 @16" O.C.

GRADE

7'-0" MAX.

5'-6"

1'-2" 1'-2"

1'-2"

3" CLR.

1'-0"

1'-8" 1'-2"

5'-4"

Detail 35(d).   Stem height 7'0".

Notes · Drawings · Ideas

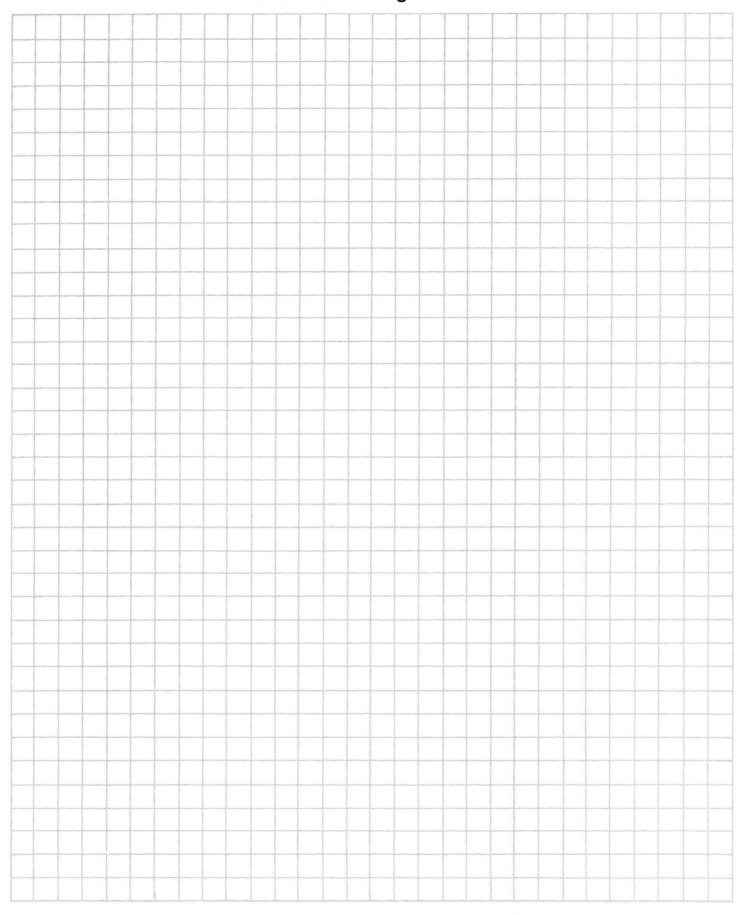

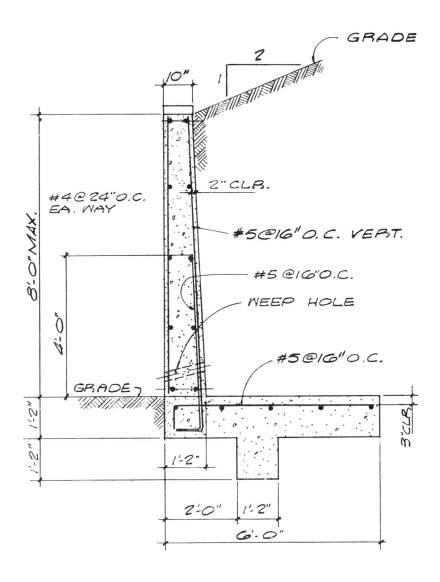

GRADE

2

1

10"

#4@24"O.C.
EA. WAY

8'-0"MAX.

6'-0"

2"CLR.

#5@16" O.C. VERT.

#5 @16'O.C.

WEEP HOLE

#5@16" O.C.

GRADE

3"CLR.

1'-2"

1'-2"

1'-2"

1'-2"

2'-0"

1'-2"

6'-0"

Detail 35(e). Stem height 8'0".

Notes · Drawings · Ideas

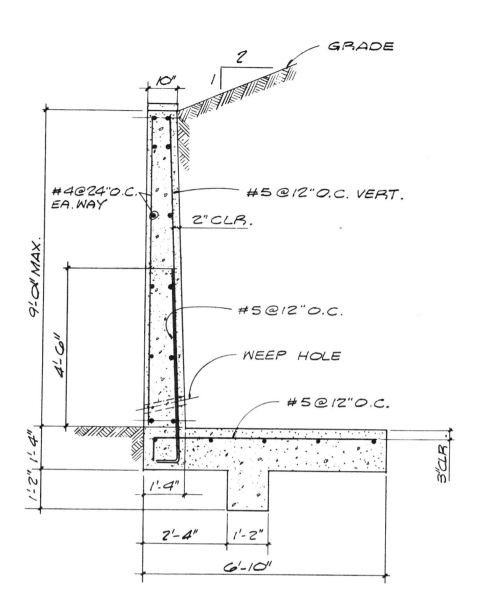

GRADE

2

1

10"

#4@24"O.C.
EA.WAY

#5 @12"O.C. VERT.

2"CLR.

#5@12"O.C.

WEEP HOLE

#5@12"O.C.

9'-0" MAX.

4'-6"

1'-4"

1'-2"

3"CLR.

1'-4"

2'-4"

1'-2"

6'-10"

] **Detail 35(f).** Stem height 9'0".

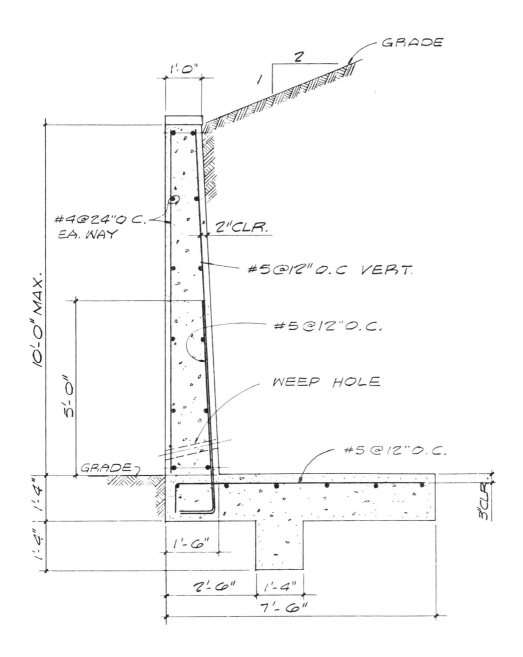

GRADE

1'-0"

2
1

#4@24"O.C. EA. WAY

2"CLR.

#5@12"O.C VERT.

#5@12"O.C.

WEEP HOLE

#5@12"O.C.

10'-0" MAX.

5'-0"

GRADE

1'-4"

3"CLR.

1'-6"

2'-6"   1'-4"

7'-6"

Detail 35(g). Stem height 10′0″. ″

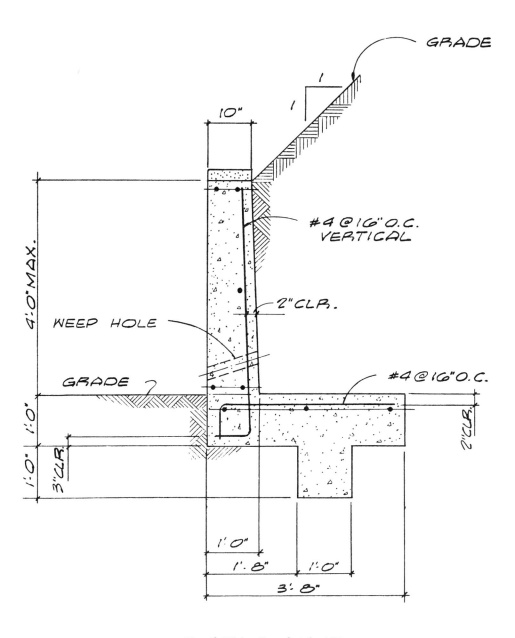

GRADE

10"

4'0" MAX.

#4 @ 16" O.C.
VERTICAL

2" CLR.

WEEP HOLE

GRADE

#4 @ 16" O.C.

2" CLR.

1'0" 1'0"

3" CLR.

1' 0"

1'. 8"   1' 0"

3'. 8"

Detail 36(a).   Stem height 4'0".

Detail 36. Sections of concrete retaining walls with soil at the interior face of the stem. The wall retains a sloping grade of one horizontal to one vertical and no surcharge. The wall dimensions and reinforcing steel size and spacing are determined by calculation. Two #4 horizontal continuous reinforcing bars are placed at the top and the bottom of the wall stem. The minimum horizontal reinforcement in the stem wall and footing is #4 at 24" o.c. A 3" dia. galvanized iron pipe spaced at 8'0" o.c. is placed at the base of the stem to act as a weep hole. The cement cap at the top of the wall is optional. The walls are designed for 80 lb per cu ft equivalent fluid pressure and a maximum soil pressure of 1500 lb per sq ft. The resultant of the forces passes through the middle $\frac{1}{3}$ of the wall footing. The walls are designed to resist sliding and overturning. The overturning safety factor is 1.5. The concrete design stress is $f'c = 2000$ psi.

Notes · Drawings · Ideas

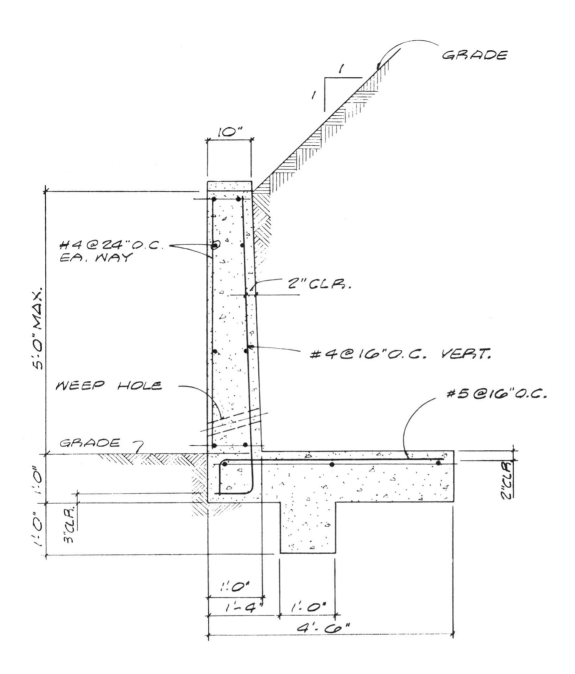

GRADE

10"

#4@24"O.C. EA. WAY

2"CLR.

#4@16"O.C. VERT.

#5 @16"O.C.

WEEP HOLE

5'0" MAX.

GRADE

2"CLR.

1'-0"

1'-0"

3"CLR.

1'-0"

1'-4"

1'-0"

4'-6"

Detail 36(b). Stem height 5'0".

Notes ▪ Drawings ▪ Ideas

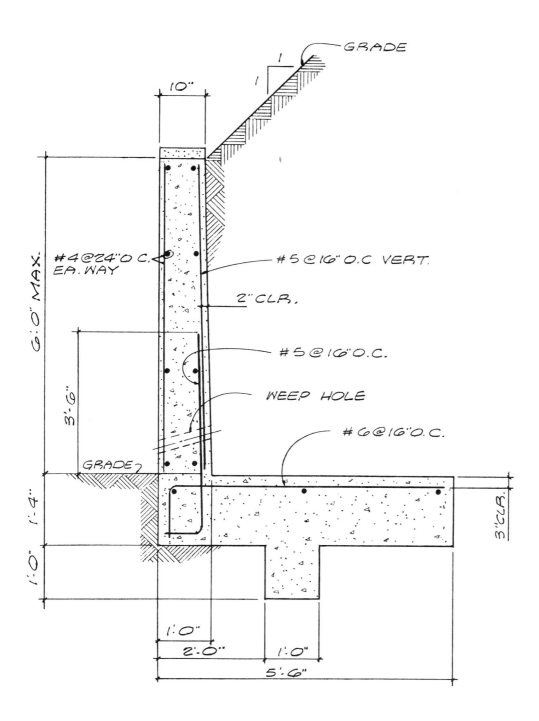

Detail 36(c). Stem height 6′0″.

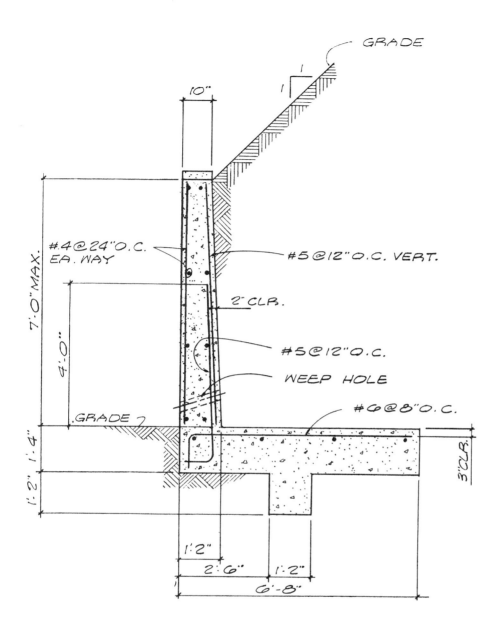

Detail 36(d). Stem height 7′0″.

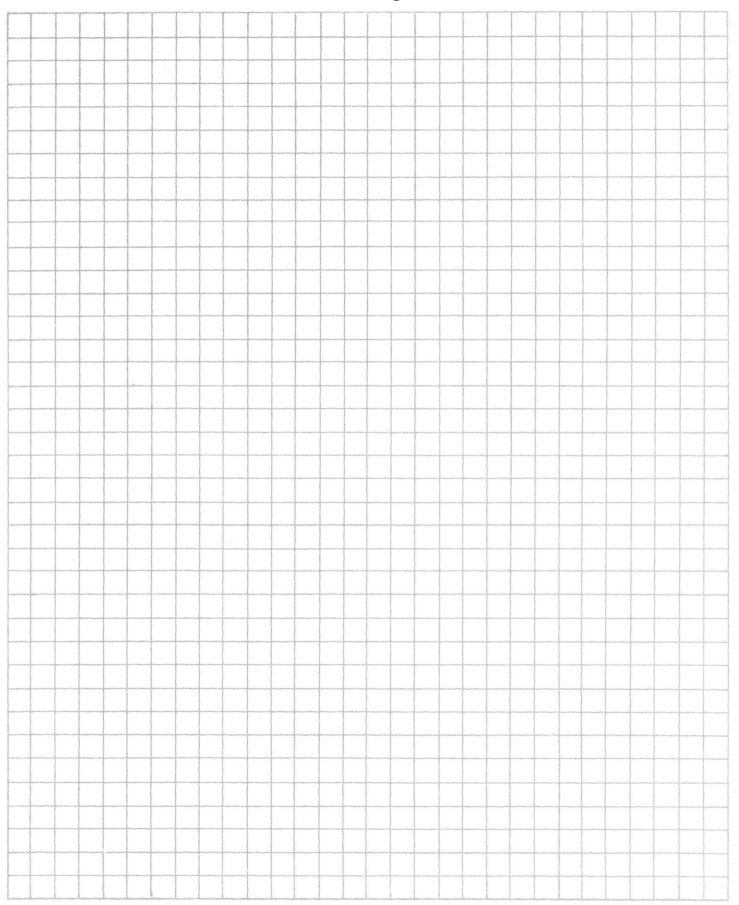

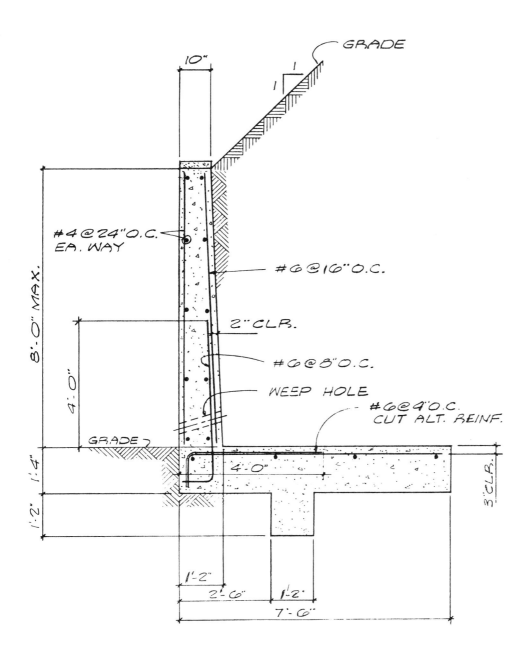

GRADE

10"

#4 @ 24" O.C.
EA. WAY

#6 @ 16" O.C.

2" CLR.

#6 @ 8" O.C.

WEEP HOLE

#6 @ 4" O.C.
CUT ALT. REINF.

8'-0" MAX.

4'-0"

GRADE

1'-4"

1'-2"

3" CLR.

4'-0"

1'-2"

2'-6"

1'-2"

7'-6"

Detail 36(e). Stem height 8'0".

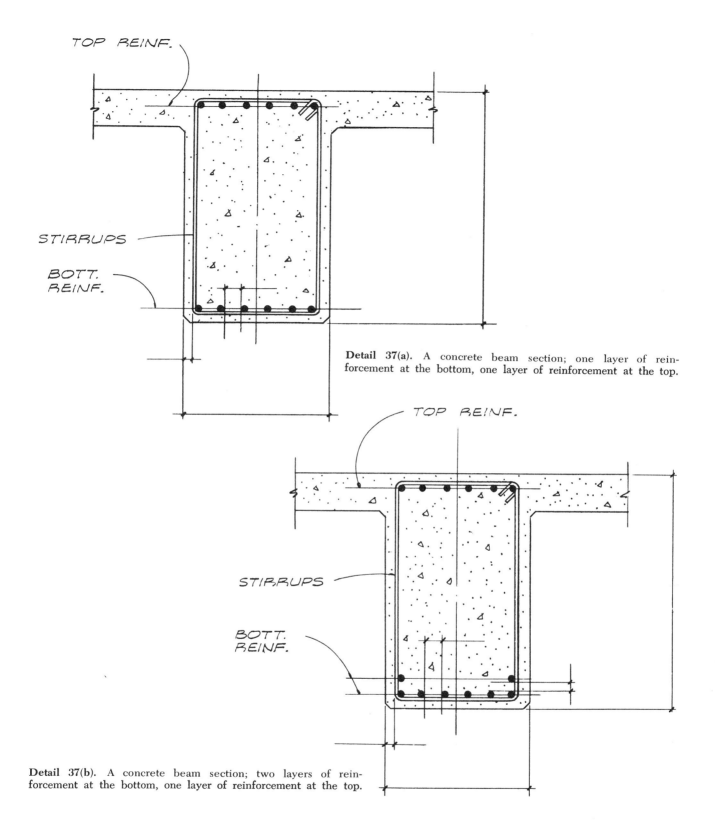

TOP REINF.

STIRRUPS

BOTT. REINF.

Detail 37(a). A concrete beam section; one layer of reinforcement at the bottom, one layer of reinforcement at the top.

TOP REINF.

STIRRUPS

BOTT. REINF.

Detail 37(b). A concrete beam section; two layers of reinforcement at the bottom, one layer of reinforcement at the top.

Detail 37. Sections of concrete beams with various combinations of top and bottom reinforcing steel. The minimum horizontal clear distance between reinforcing bars is the diameter of the bar, or 1⅓ times the maximum size of the coarse aggregate or not less than 1″. The minimum concrete coverage of the reinforcing steel is 1½″. The concrete cover over the reinforcing steel may be increased to obtain a higher fire rating of the beam. The clear vertical distance between layers of reinforcement is the diameter of the bar, or 1⅓ times the size of the coarse aggregate or not less than 1″. The bars of each layer should be placed directly in line with each other.

Notes · Drawings · Ideas

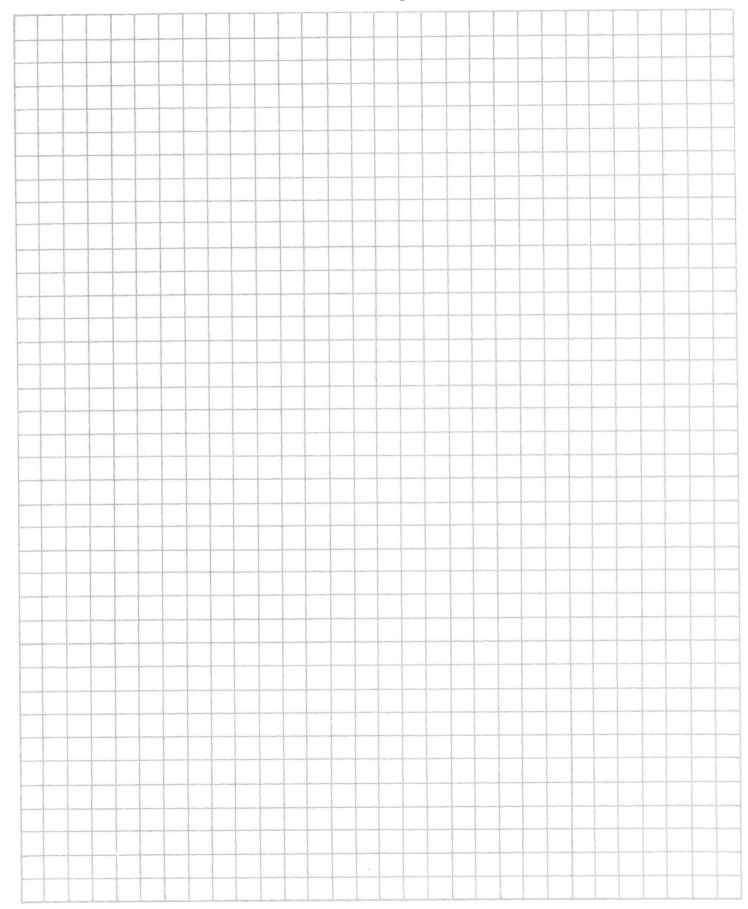

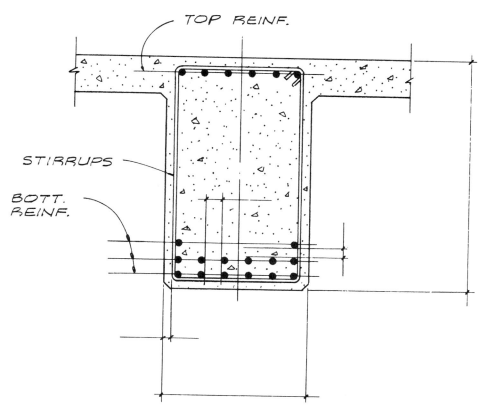

Detail 37(c). A concrete beam section; three layers of reinforcement at the bottom, one layer of reinforcement at the top.

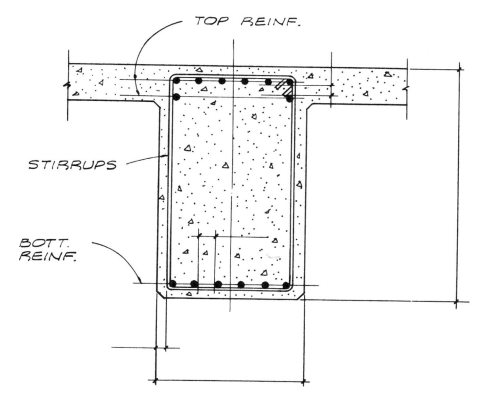

Detail 37(d). A concrete beam section; one layer of reinforcement at the bottom, two layers of reinforcement at the top.

Notes ▪ Drawings ▪ Ideas

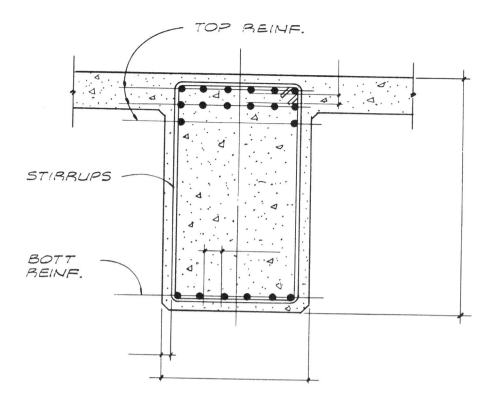

Detail 37(e). A concrete beam section; one layer of reinforcement at the bottom, three layers of reinforcement at the top.

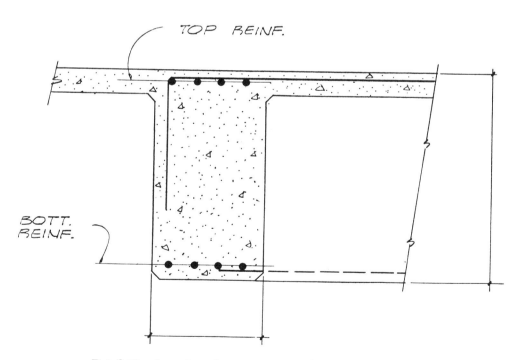

Detail 38. A section of an intersection of two concrete beams. The top end reinforcing bars of the intersecting beam are bent down into the supporting beam as shown. The bottom bars of the intersecting beam extend a minimum of 6″ into the supporting beam.

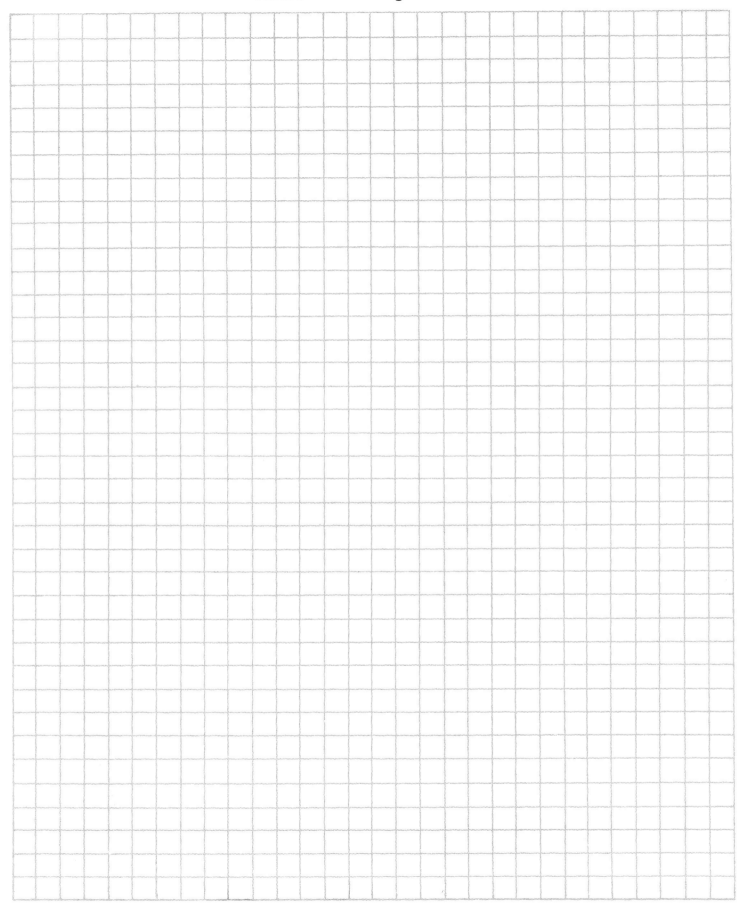

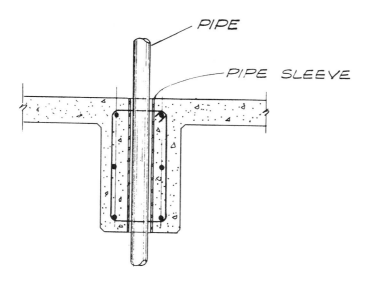

PIPE

PIPE SLEEVE

Detail 39(a). A section of a pipe passing vertically through a concrete beam. The pipe is sleeved. Extra reinforcing bars are added to the beam to compensate for the concrete cross-sectional area removed by the pipe. The amount of added reinforcing bars and stirrups is determined by calculating the bending and shear in the reduced beam section.

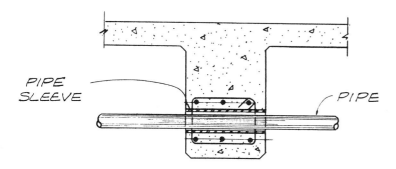

PIPE SLEEVE

PIPE

Detail 39(b). A section of a pipe passing horizontally through a concrete beam. The pipe is sleeved. Extra reinforcing bars are added to the beam to compensate for the concrete cross-sectional area removed by the pipe. The amount of added reinforcing bars and stirrups is determined by calculating the bending and shear in the reduced beam section.

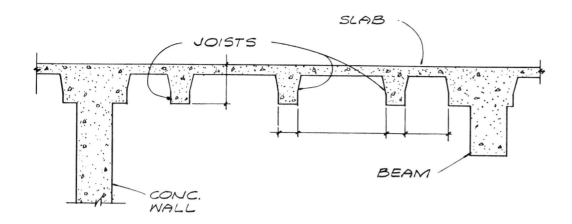

Detail 40. A section of a concrete slab and joists formed by inverted metal pans and wood soffits. The depth of the joists is varied by adjusting the height of the wood soffit form. The slab thickness depends on the load and the span between the joists. The ends of the concrete joists can be flared 2″ on each side for a length of 36″ to increase the width in order to reduce the shear stress. The width of the joist depends on the nominal width of the wood soffit form used. The pan form widths vary in increments of 10″, 15″, 20″, 30″. The slab and joist reinforcements are not shown.

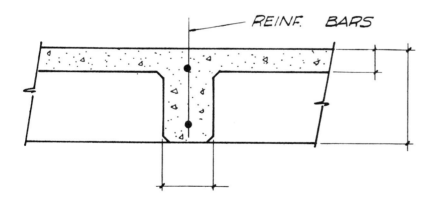

Detail 41. A section of a concrete pan joist bridge. The number of rows of bridging is determined by the local building code. The depth and width of the bridge section are equal to the depth and width of the joists.

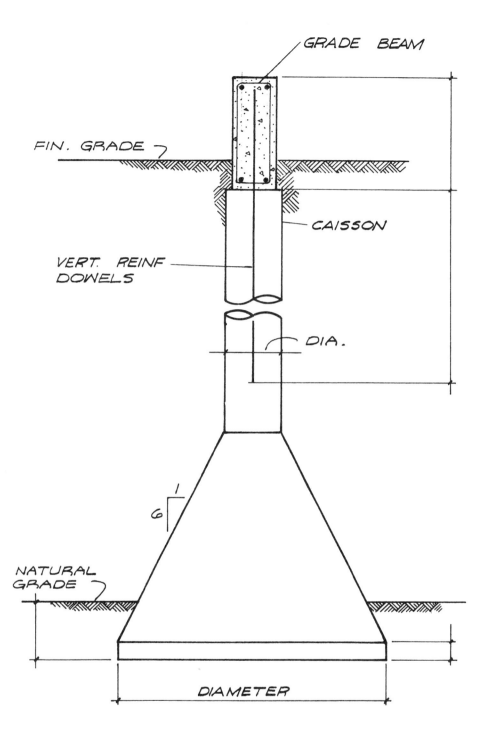

Detail 42. An elevation of a concrete caisson supporting a concrete grade beam. The grade beam is connected to the caisson shaft with vertical reinforcing dowels. The caisson shaft diameter depends on the length required to reach acceptable bearing soil below grade. The bell diameter at the base of the caisson is determined by the load on the caisson and the allowable bearing capacity of the soil. The depth of the bell base into the bearing soil is determined by calculation and the local building code. See Details 43(a) and (b).

Notes ▪ Drawings ▪ Ideas

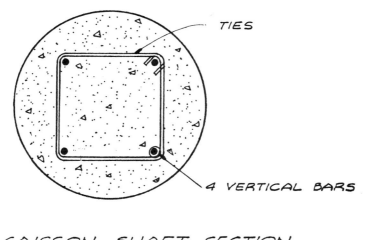

TIES

4 VERTICAL BARS

CAISSON SHAFT SECTION

Detail 43(a). A plan section of a caisson shaft. The shaft is reinforced with a minimum of four vertical bars tied together in the same way as required for a rectangular concrete column. See Detail 49(a).

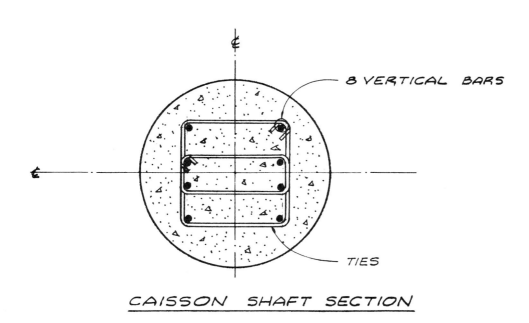

8 VERTICAL BARS

TIES

CAISSON SHAFT SECTION

Detail 43(b). A plan section of a caisson shaft. The shaft is reinforced with eight vertical bars tied together in the same way as required for a rectangular column. See Detail 49(a). The arrangement of the vertical reinforcement permits the caisson shaft to resist axial and bending loads.

Notes ▪ Drawings ▪ Ideas

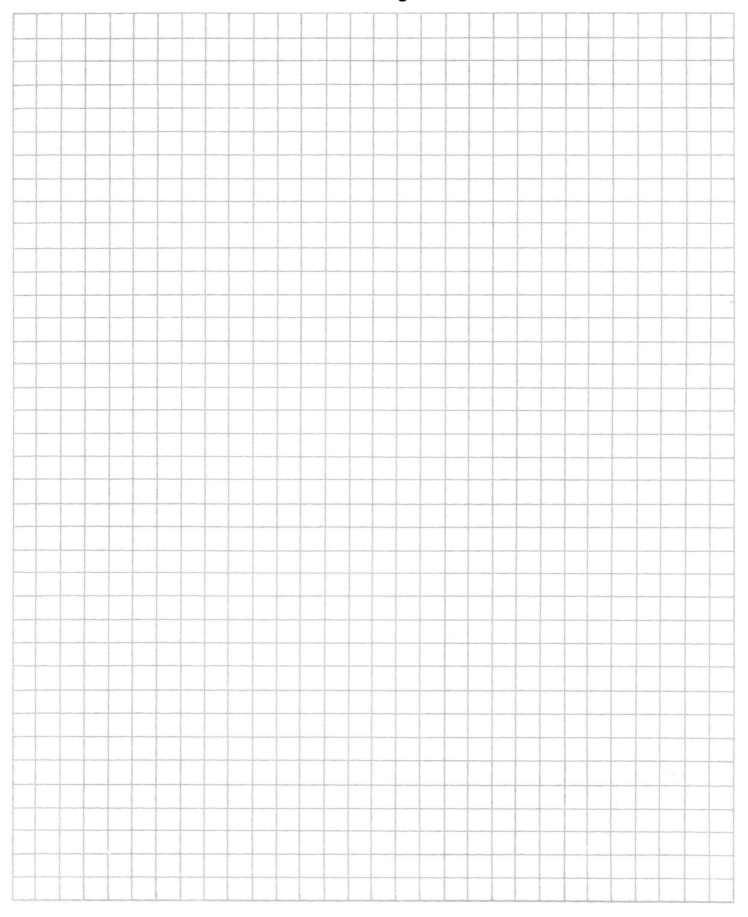

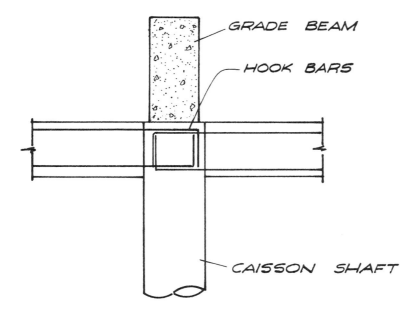

Detail 44(a). An elevation of concrete tie beams connected to the top of a caisson shaft. The tie beams restrain the caisson shaft laterally in each direction. The tie beam reinforcing bars are lapped and bent at the top of the caisson shaft as shown. See Detail 44(b).

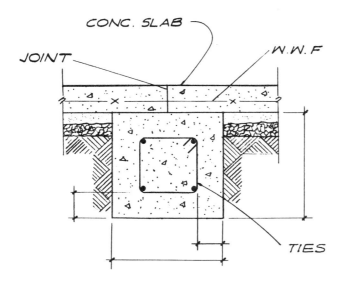

Detail 44(b). A section of a concrete tie beam. See Detail 44(a). The minimum reinforcement in the tie beam is four #4 bars and #2 ties spaced the same as for a rectangular concrete column. See Detail 49(a).

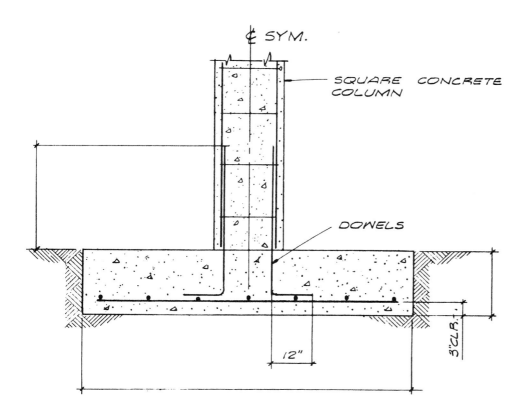

Detail 45. A concrete spread footing supporting a rectangular concrete column. The column is connected to the spread footing by reinforcing dowels. The reinforcing dowels lap the column vertical reinforcement 40 bar diameters or not less than 24″. The size and spacing of the footing reinforcement are determined by calculation. The depth and the area of the spread footing depend on the soil conditions.

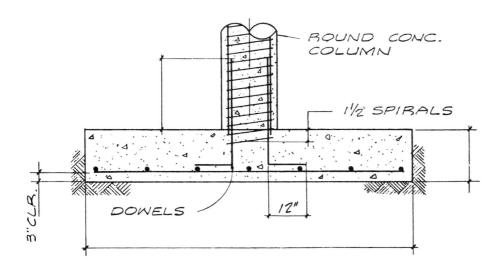

Detail 46. A concrete spread footing supporting a round concrete column. The column is connected to the spread footing by reinforcing dowels. The reinforcing dowels lap the column vertical reinforcement 40 bar diameters or not less than 24″. The column spirals extend 1½ turns into the top of the spread footing. The size and spacing of the footing reinforcement are determined by calculation. The depth and the area of the spread footing depend on the soil conditions.

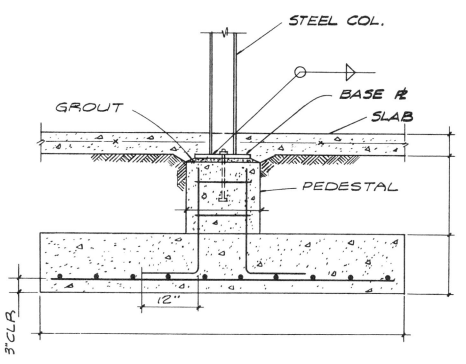

Detail 47(a). A concrete spread footing supporting a wide-flange steel column. The column base plate is set on a layer of grout. The column load is transferred to the spread footing by a rectangular concrete pedestal. The height of the pedestal is determined by the depth of the footing into the soil. The pedestal is reinforced with a minimum of four vertical bars tied together in the same way as required for a rectangular concrete column. See Detai 49(a). The size and spacing of the footing reinforcement are determined by calculation. The depth and the area of the spread footing depend on the soil conditions.

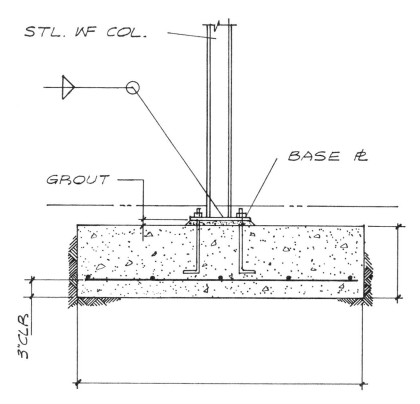

Detail 47(b). A concrete spread footing supporting a wide-flange steel column. The column base plate is set on a layer of grout. The size and spacing of the footing reinforcement are determined by calculation. The depth and the area of the spread footing depend on the soil conditions.

157

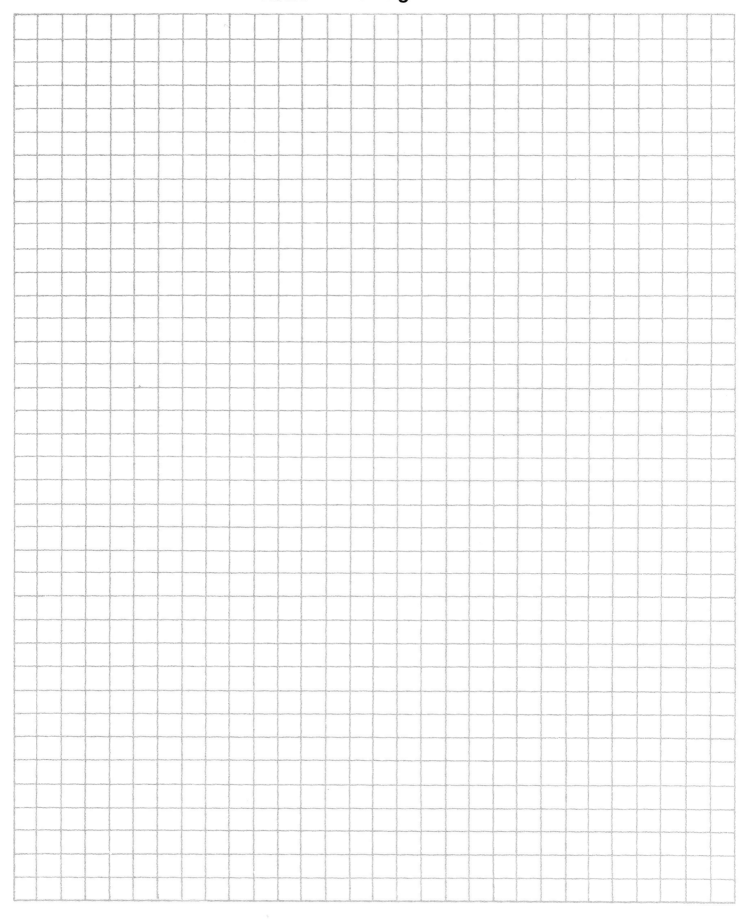

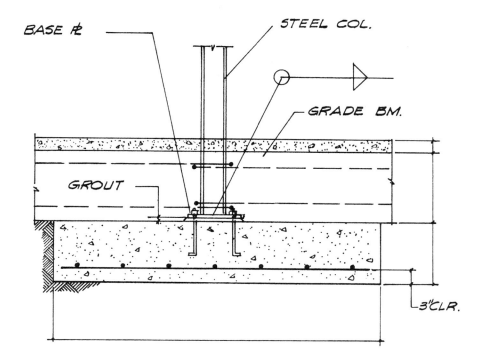

BASE ℞

STEEL COL.

GRADE BM.

GROUT

3"CLR.

Detail 47(c). A concrete spread footing supporting a wide-flange steel column through a concrete grade beam. The column base plate is set on a layer of grout. The concrete grade beam is poured around the base of the steel column. The grade beam reinforcing bars are bent 90° around the column as shown. The grade beam permits the column to resist axial loads and bending in the direction of the grade beam. The size and spacing of the footing and grade beam reinforcement are determined by calculation. The depth and the area of the spread footing depend on the soil conditions.

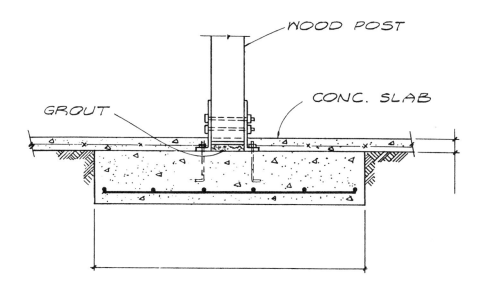

WOOD POST

CONC. SLAB

GROUT

Detail 47(d). A concrete spread footing supporting a wood post. The size and spacing of the footing reinforcement are determined by calculation. The size and the depth of the spread footing depend on the soil conditions.

Notes ▪ Drawings ▪ Ideas

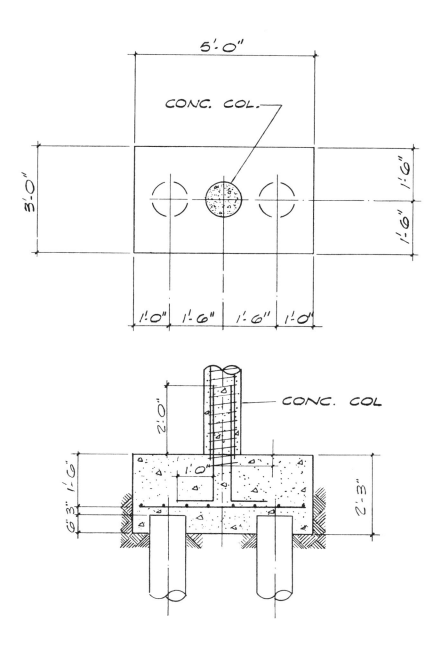

Detail 48(a). Two piles.

Detail 48. Concrete pile cap plans and sections. The pile cap may be used for concrete, wood, or steel piles. The pile spacing shown on each plan is for a 12″ dia. concrete pile. The spacing between piles depends on the size of the pile. Larger diameter piles require an increased pile spacing. A total friction pile cluster capacity depends on the pile size, the number and spacing of the piles, and the soil conditions. The pile cap may support a steel or a concrete column. The concrete column shown is connected to the pile cap by reinforcing dowels. The reinforcing dowels lap the column vertical reinforcement 40 bar diameters or not less than 24″. The column spirals extend 1½ turns into the top of the pile cap. The size and spacing of the pile cap reinforcement are determined by calculation.

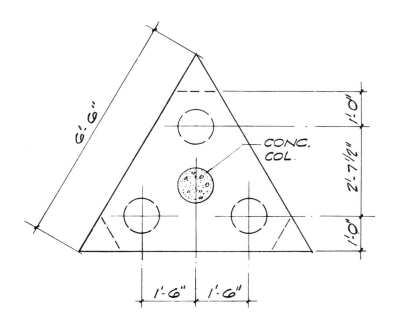

CONC.
COL.

6'-6"

2'-7½"

1'-0"

1'-0"

1'-6" 1'-6"

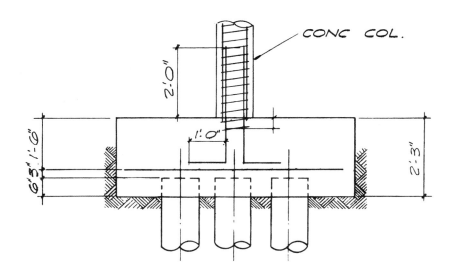

CONC COL.

2'-0"

1'-0"

6'-5" 1'-6"

2'-3"

Detail 48(b). Three piles.

Notes ▪ Drawings ▪ Ideas

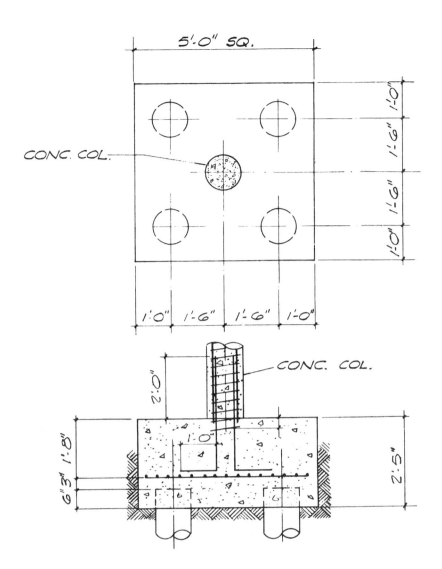

5'-0" SQ.

CONC. COL.

1'-0" 1'-6" 1'-6" 1'-0"

1'-0" 1'-6" 1'-6" 1'-0"

CONC. COL.

2'-0"

1'-0"

6" 3" 1'-8"

2'-5"

Detail 48(c). Four piles.

Notes ▪ Drawings ▪ Ideas

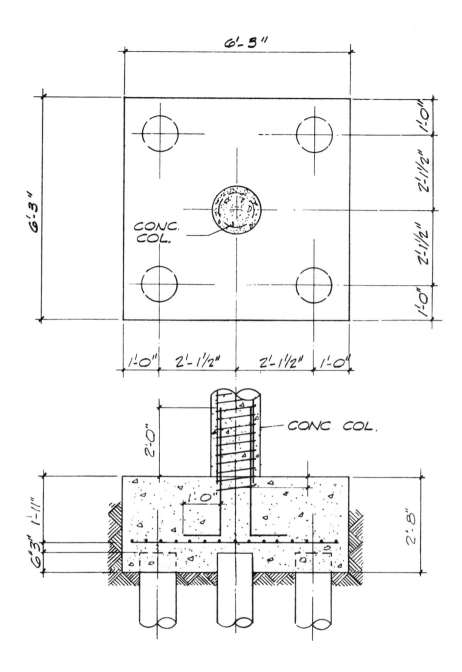

Detail 48(d). Five piles.

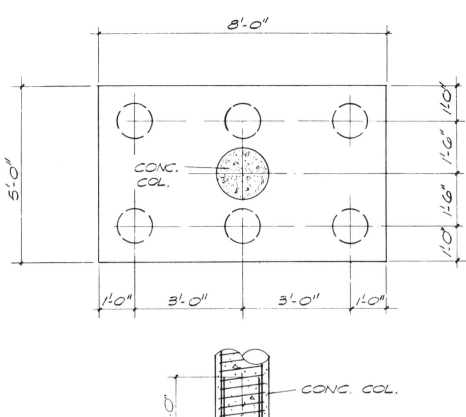

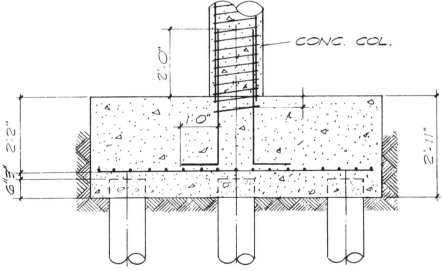

Detail 48(e). Six piles.

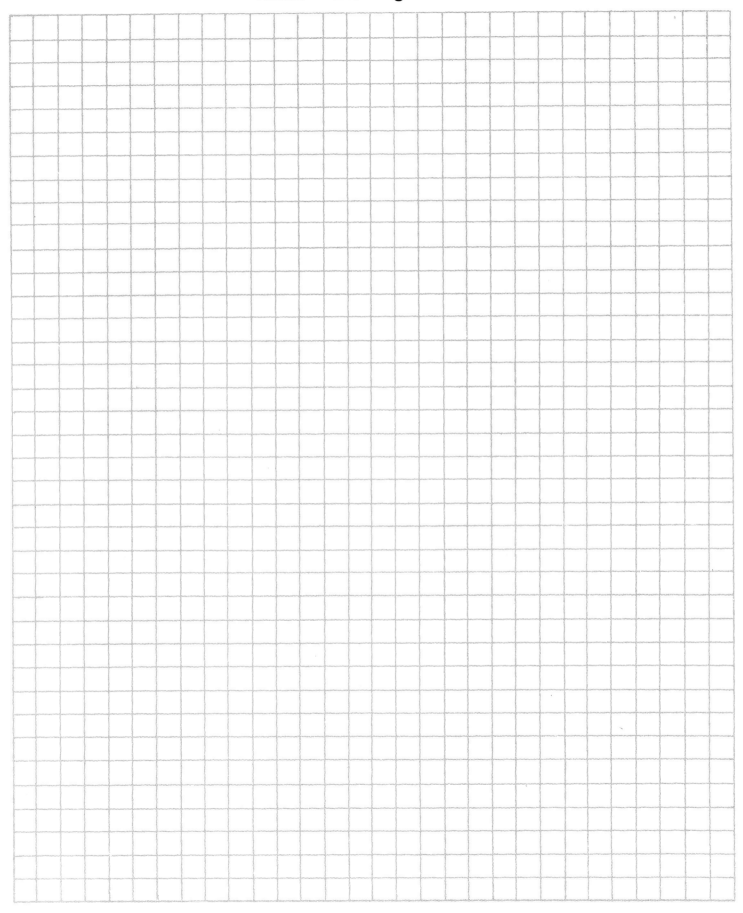

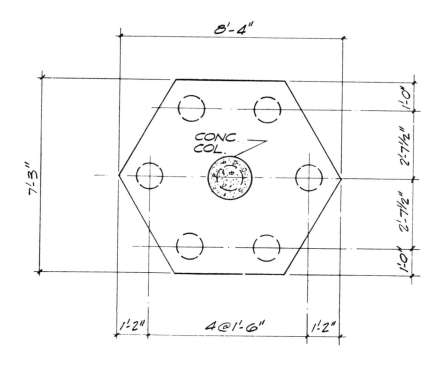

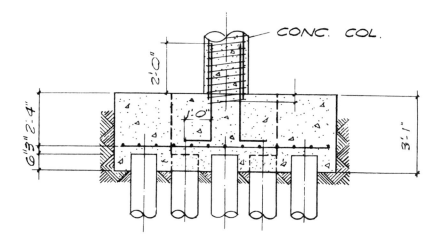

Detail 48(f). Seven piles.

Notes ▪ Drawings ▪ Ideas

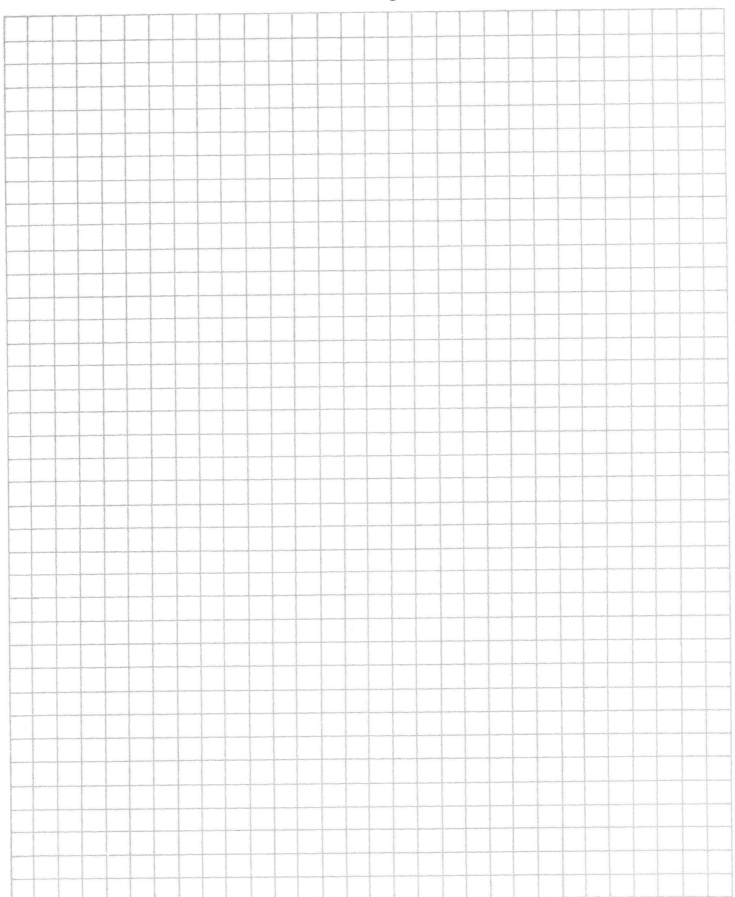

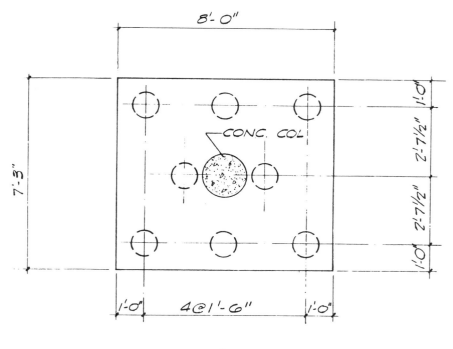

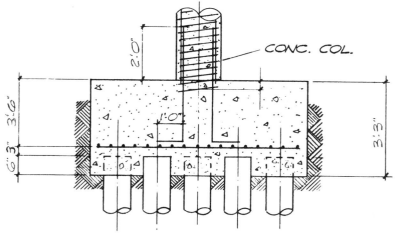

Detail 48(g).   Eight piles.

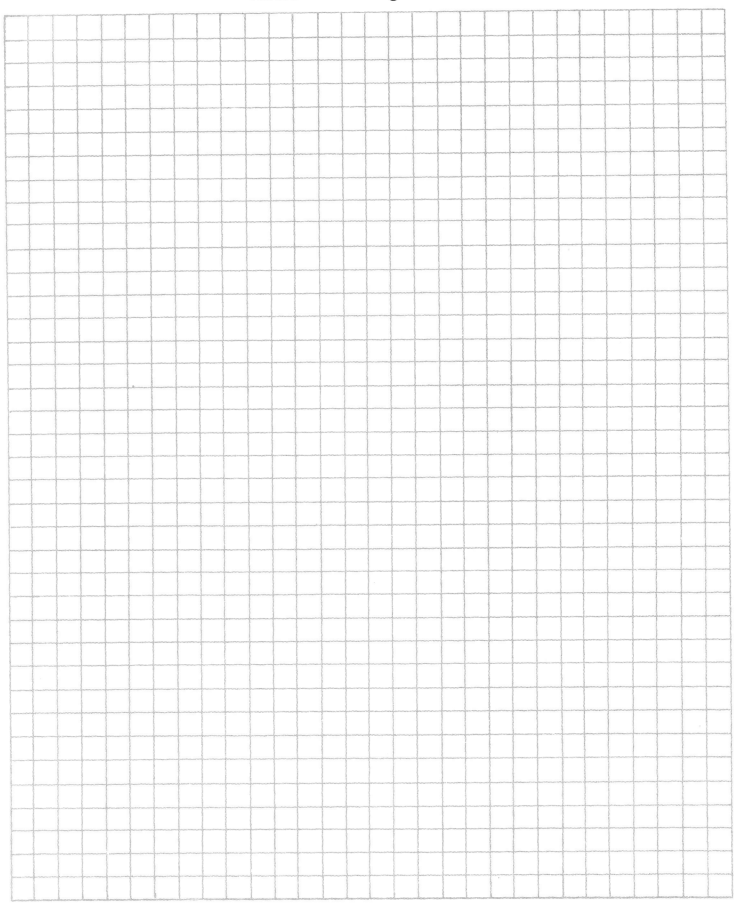

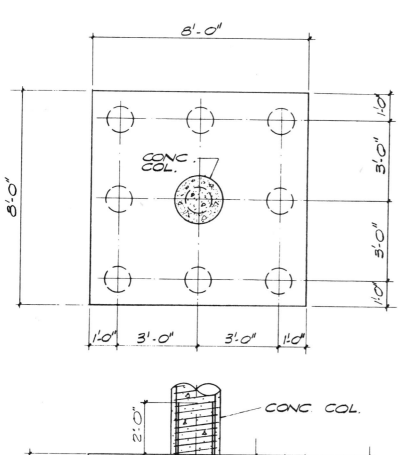

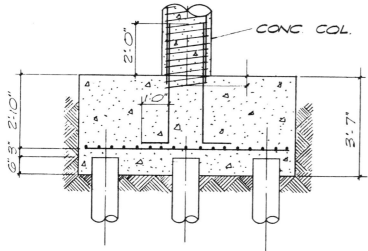

Detail 48(h). Nine piles.

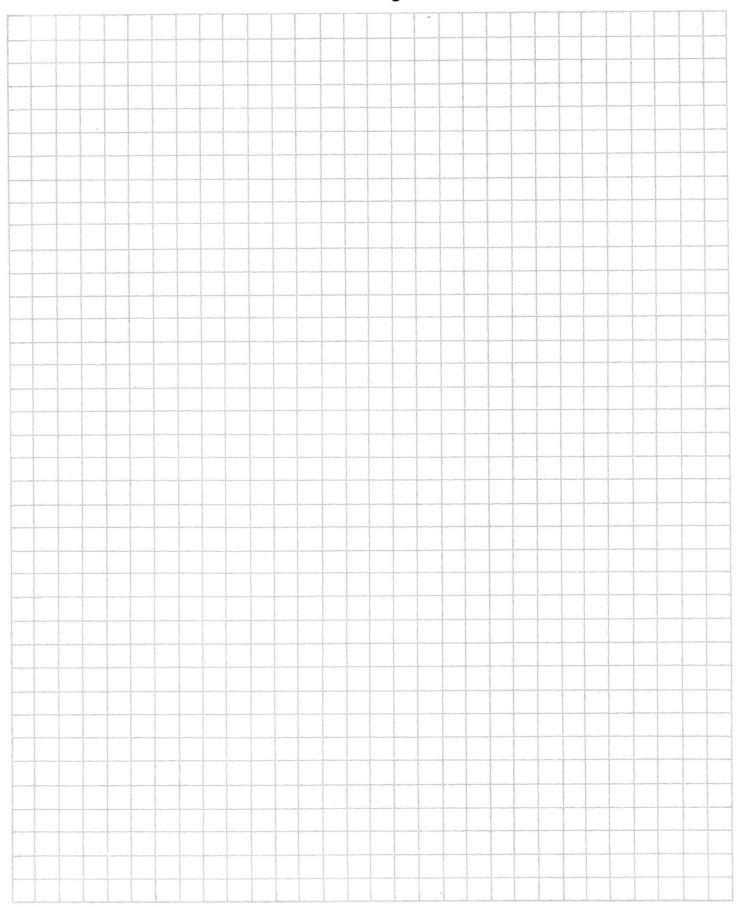

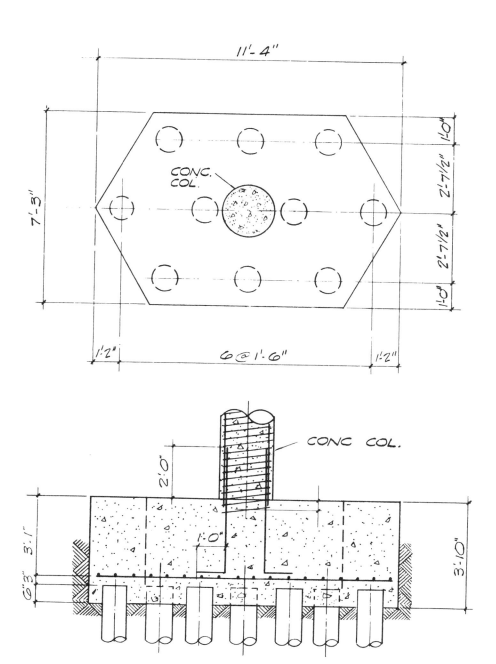

Detail 48(i). Ten piles.

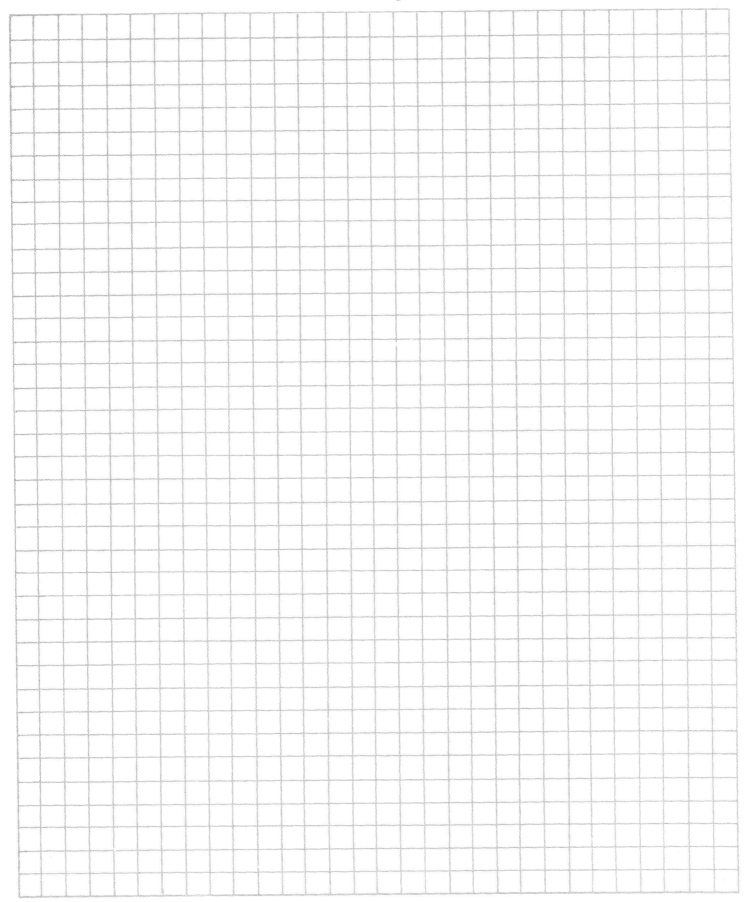

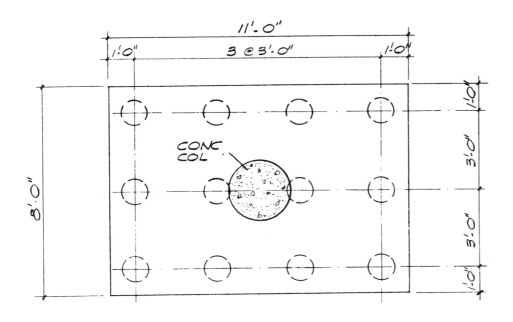

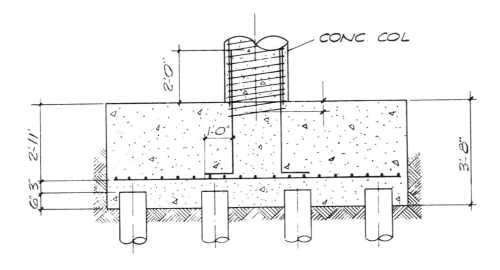

Detail 48(j).   Twelve piles.

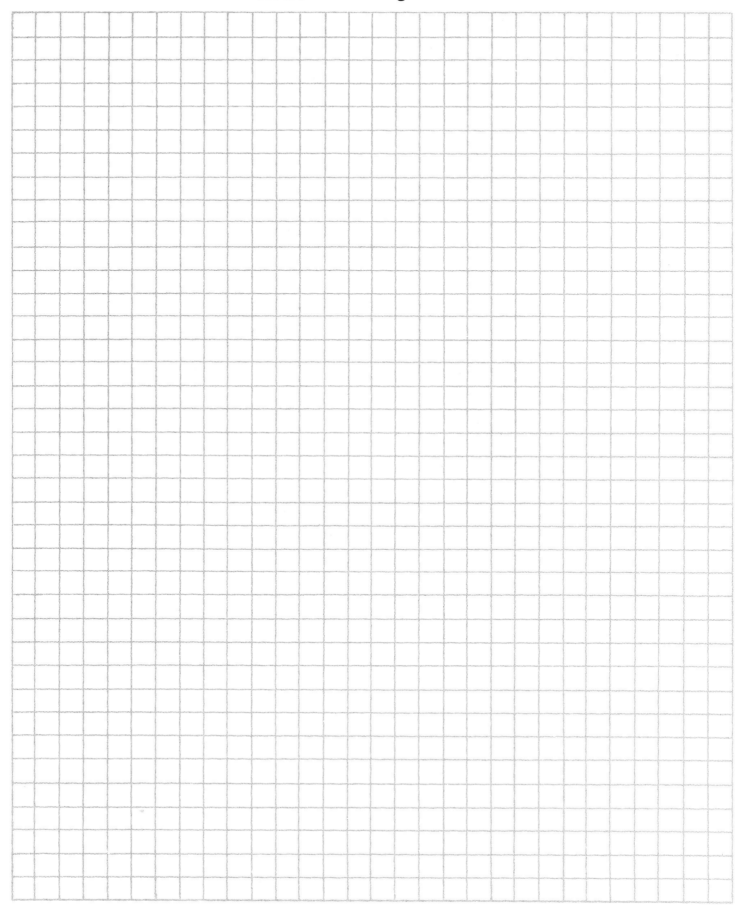

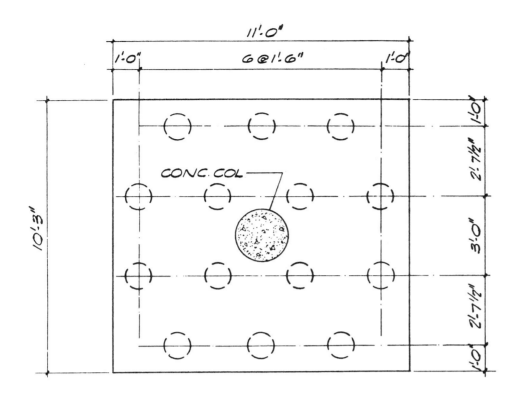

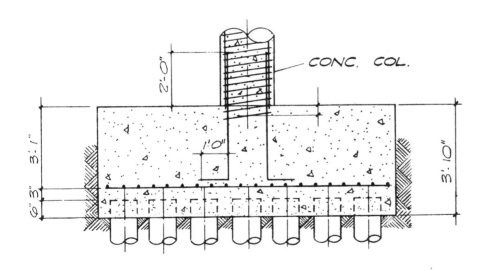

Detail 48(k). Fourteen piles.

Notes ▪ Drawings ▪ Ideas

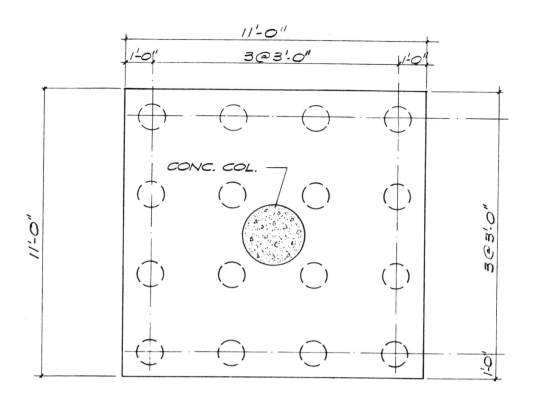

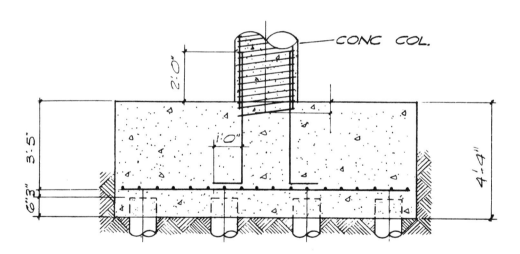

Detail 48(l). Sixteen piles.

Notes ▪ Drawings ▪ Ideas

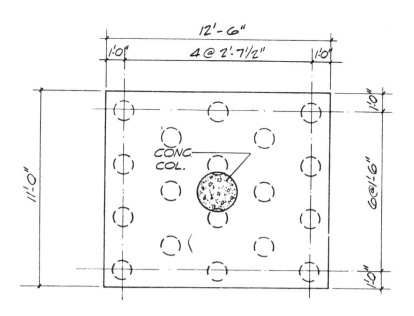

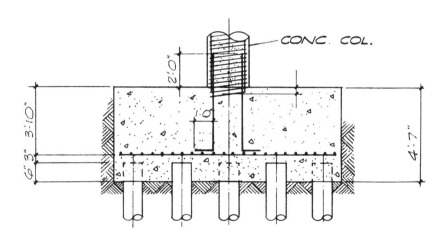

Detail 48(m).   Eighteen piles.

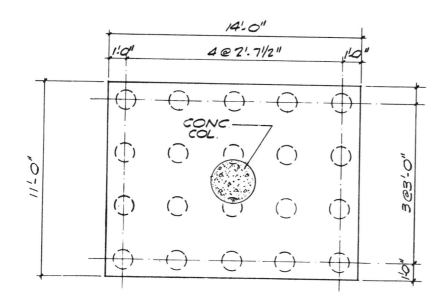

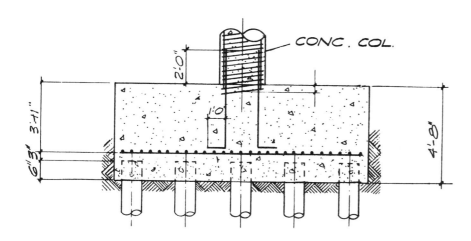

Detail 48(n). Twenty piles.

Notes ▪ Drawings ▪ Ideas

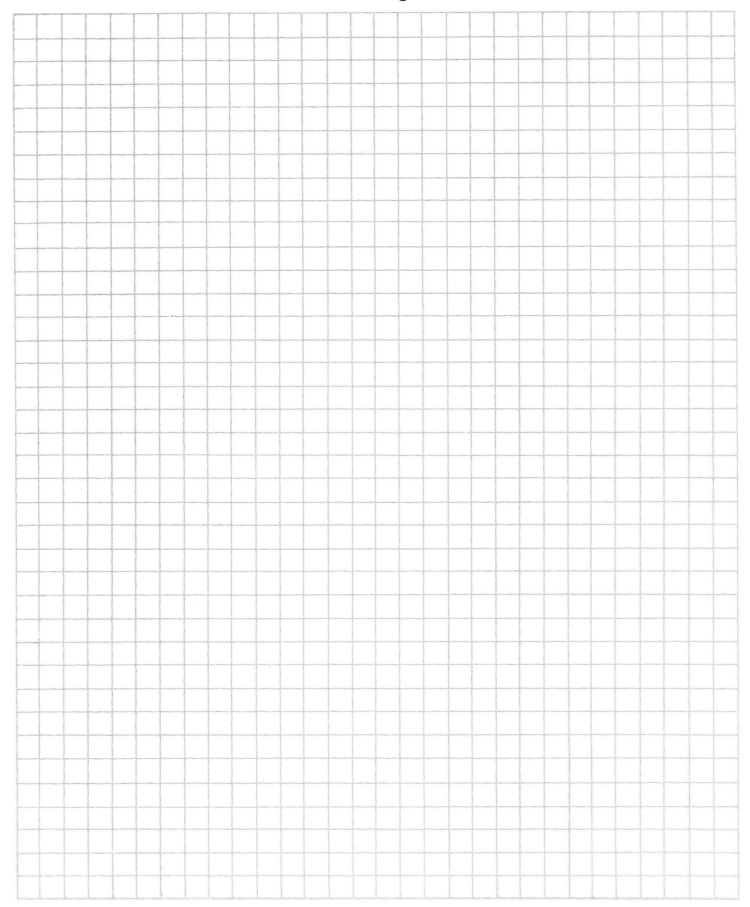

<u>4 VERT BARS</u>

<u>6 VERT BARS</u>

<u>8 VERT BARS</u>

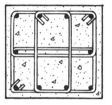

<u>10 VERT BARS</u>

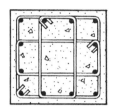

<u>12 VERT BARS</u>

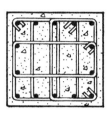

<u>14 VERT BARS</u>

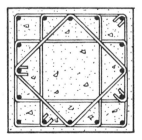

<u>16 VERT BARS</u>

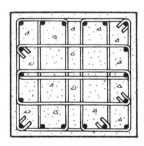

<u>18 VERT BARS</u>

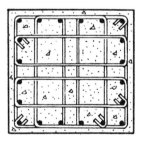

<u>20 VERT BARS</u>

Detail 49(a). Plan sections of square or rectangular concrete columns. The number of vertical reinforcing bars are shown for each particular column. The vertical reinforcement in square or rectangular concrete columns is not less than 1% or more than 4% of the column cross section, or not less than four #4 reinforcing bars. Every vertical reinforcing bar is secured firmly in place and is laterally supported by a 90° bend of a reinforcing tie bar. The minimum tie bar is ¼″ dia. rod. The maximum tie-bar spacing is 48 tie-bar diameters, 16 vertical-bar diameters, or not more than the least dimension of the column. The minimum distance between the vertical reinforcing bars is 2½ times the diameter of the vertical bar, or not less than 1½″ clear. Pairs of reinforcing bars of a lapped splice may be in contact with each other. The minimum clear concrete cover of the reinforcement is 1½″.

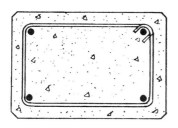

4 VERTICAL BARS

Detail 49(a).

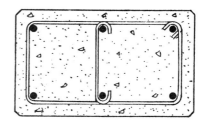

6 VERTICAL BARS

Detail 49(a).

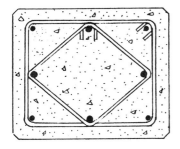

8 VERTICAL BARS

Detail 49(a).

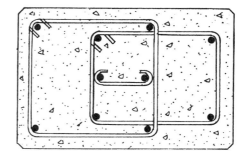

10 VERTICAL BARS

Detail 49(a).

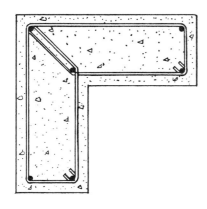

CONC. COL. SECTION

Detail 49(b). A plan section of a wall corner used as a concrete column. The reinforcement is placed as shown, and as required in Detail 49a. The capacity of the column depends on the cross-sectional area, the amount of vertical reinforcement, and the column slenderness ratio.

Notes ▪ Drawings ▪ Ideas

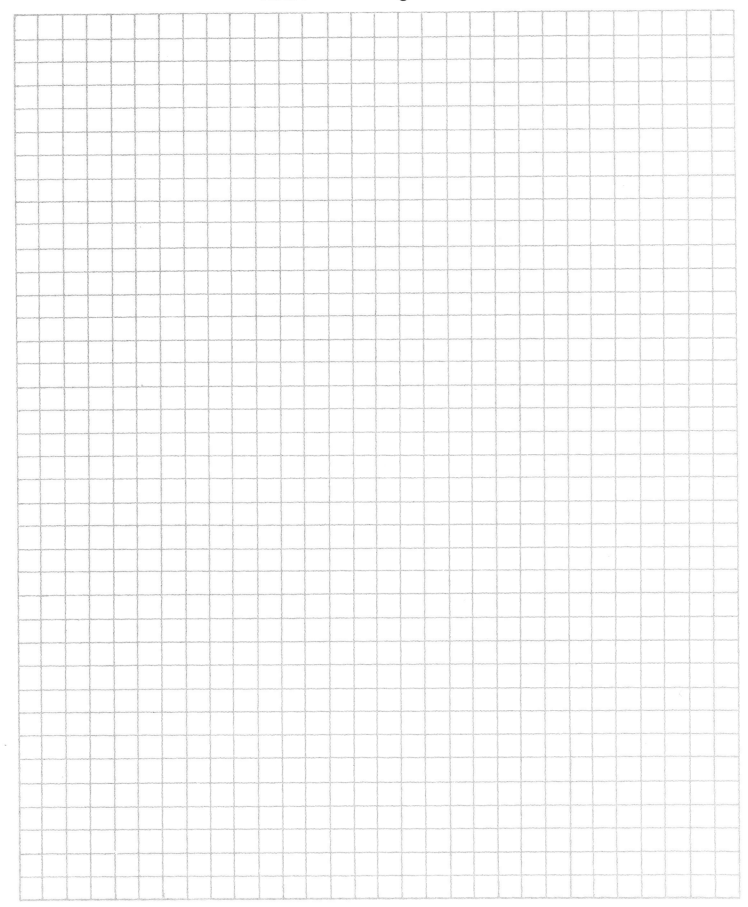

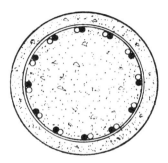

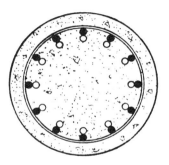

Detail 50(a). A plan section of a round concrete column. The minimum column diameter is 12″. The vertical reinforcement in a round concrete column is not less than 1% or not more than 8% of the column cross section, or not less than five #4 reinforcing bars. The vertical reinforcing bars are held in place by the column spiral steel. The spiral reinforcement consists of evenly spaced continuous rod. The minimum spiral size is ¼″ dia. for rolled bars or No. 4 U. S. Steel wire gauge for cold-drawn steel. The spiral spacing or pitch is not more than ⅙ of the column core diameter. The clear spacing between spirals is not more than 3″ or less than 1⅜″ and not less than 1½ times the maximum size of the coarse aggregate. The spirals extend 1½ turns past the top and bottom of the column. The spirals may be spliced by butt welding or by lapping 1½ turns. The spiral reinforcement is held in place by vertical metal spacers. The number of vertical spacers required depends on the spiral core diameter. The minimum distance between the vertical reinforcing bars is 2½ times the diameter of the vertical bar, or not less than 1½″ clear. Pairs of reinforcing bars of a lapped splice may be in contact with each other. The minimum clear concrete cover of the reinforcement is 1½″. The bars shown as open circles represent the reinforcing bars from the column below.

Notes ▪ Drawings ▪ Ideas

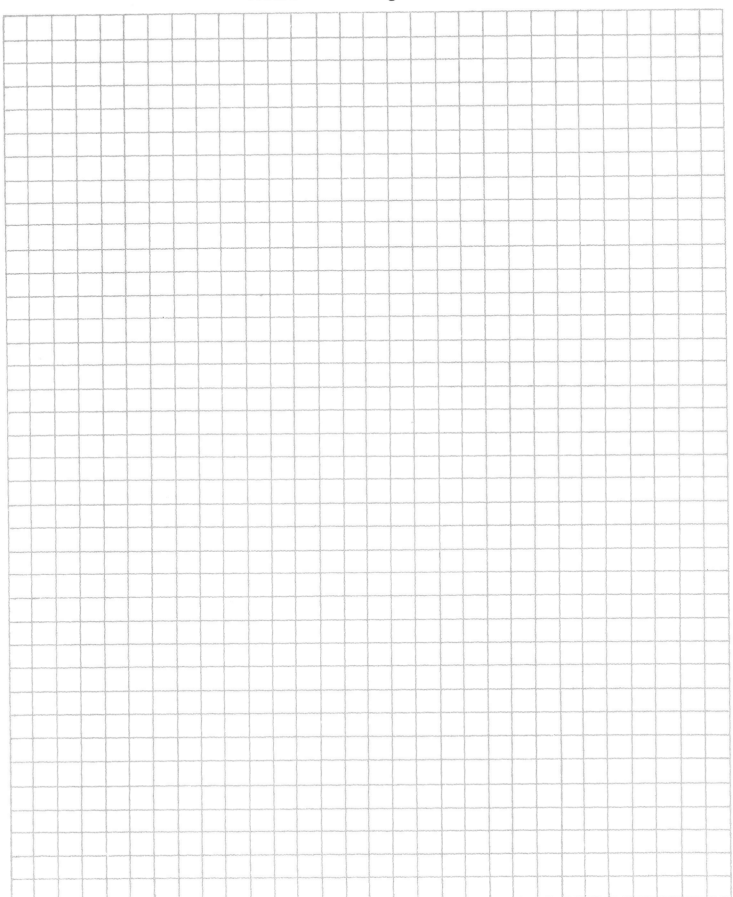

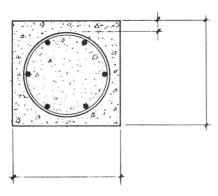

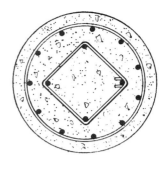

Detail 50(b). A square concrete column section with the round concrete column reinforcement arrangement. See Detail 50(a) for reinforcement requirements.

Detail 50(c). A plan section of a round concrete column with vertical reinforcing bars and spirals in the outer ring, and vertical bars and ties in the core of the column. See Details 50(a) and 49(a).

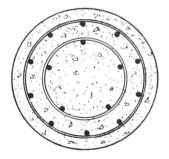

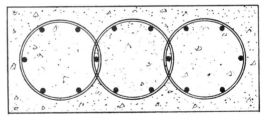

Detail 50(d). A plan section of a round concrete column with two cores of vertical reinforcement and spirals. See Detail 50(a).

Detail 50(e). A plan section of a rectangular concrete column. The reinforcing bars are arranged in three sets of round column reinforcement.

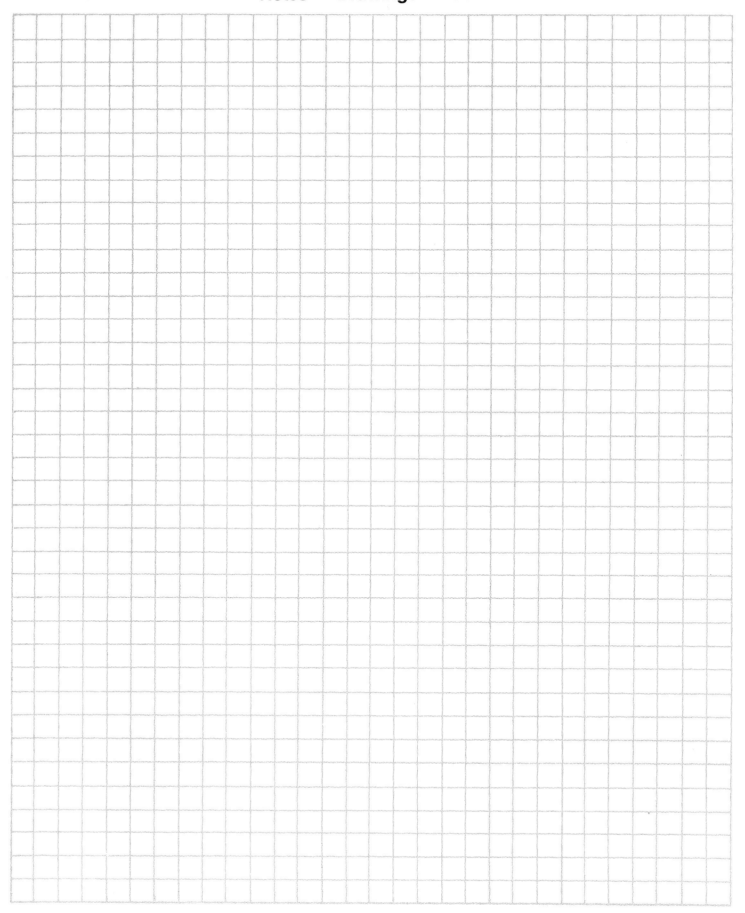

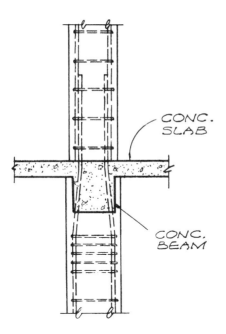

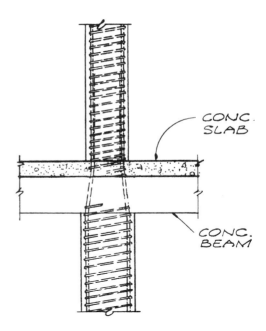

Detail 51. An elevation of a lap splice of a square or rectangular concrete column. The vertical bars may be bent at a slope of 1″ horizontally to 6″ vertically starting at the top of the slab. The lapped reinforcing bars may be in contact with each other. The length of the lap is 40 bar diameters or nor less than 24″.

Detail 52. An elevation of a lap splice of a round concrete column. The vertical bars may be bent at a slope of 1″ horizontally to 6″ vertically starting at the top of the slab. The lapped reinforcing bars may be in contact with each other. The length of the lap is 40 bar diameters or not less than 24″. The spirals are lapped 1½ turns.

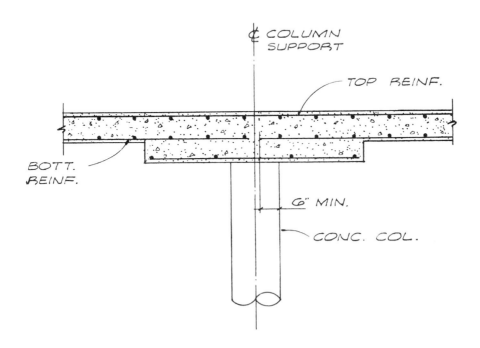

Detail 53. A section of a flat slab drop panel at a round concrete column. The slab top reinforcement is continuous across the panel in each direction. The slab bottom reinforcement extends 6″ past the edge of the panel.

Notes ▪ Drawings ▪ Ideas

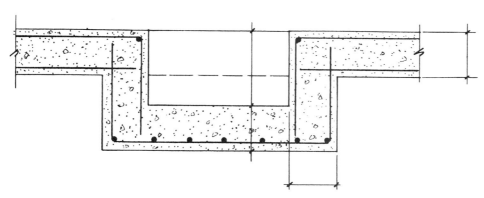

Detail 54. A section of a drop in a concrete slab. The size and spacing of the reinforcement are determined by calculation.

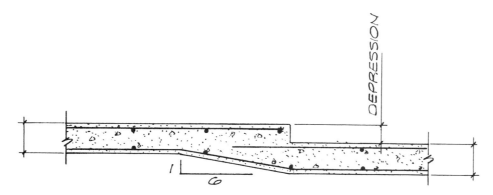

Detail 55. A section of a depression in a concrete slab. The reinforcing bars slope one vertical to six horizontal.

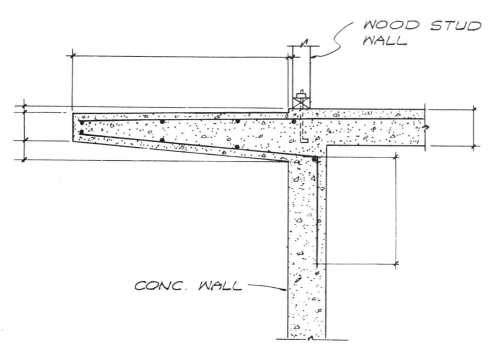

Detail 56(a). A section of a cantilevered concrete slab, a concrete wall, and a wood stud wall. The wood stud wall is set back to allow the exterior wall covering material to meet the top of the concrete slab. The exterior cantilevered slab is depressed below the interior floor slab to allow for waterproofing or flashing at the face of the stud wall. The thickness of the cantilevered slab and the size and spacing of reinforcement are determined by calculation.

Notes · Drawings · Ideas

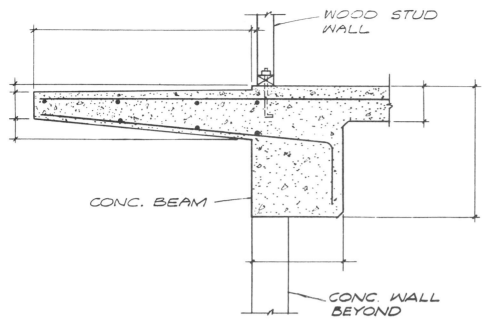

WOOD STUD WALL

CONC. BEAM

CONC. WALL BEYOND

Detail 56(b). A section of a cantilevered concrete slab, a concrete beam, and a wood stud wall. The wood stud wall is set back to allow the exterior wall covering material to meet the top of the concrete slab. The exterior cantilevered slab is depressed below the interior floor slab to allow for waterproofing or flashing at the face of the wood stud wall. The thickness of the cantilevered slab and the size and spacing of reinforcement are determined by calculation.

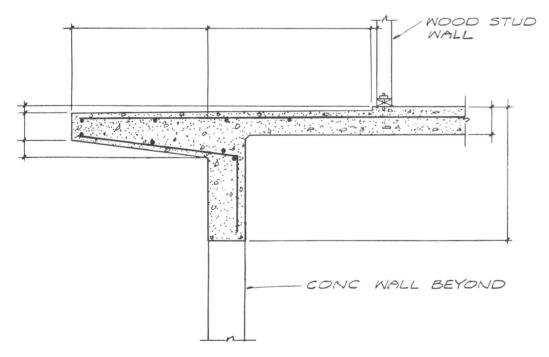

WOOD STUD WALL

CONC WALL BEYOND

Detail 56(c). A section of a cantilevered concrete slab, a concrete wall and a wood stud wall. The wood stud wall is supported by the interior concrete slab. The wood stud wall is set back to allow the exterior wall covering material to meet the top of the concrete slab. The exterior cantilevered slab is depressed below the interior floor slab to allow for waterproofing or flashing at the face of the wood stud wall. The thickness of the cantilevered slab and the size and spacing of reinforcement are determined by calculation.

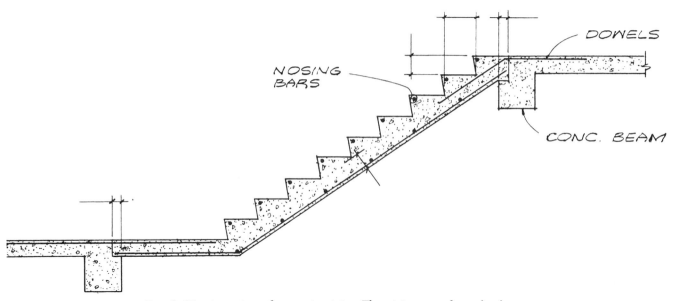

Detail 57. A section of concrete stairs. The stairs span from the beam at the top tread to the beam at the lower landing. The thickness of the slab and the size and spacing of the reinforcmeent are determined by calculation.

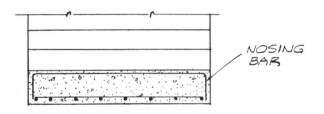

Detail 58. A section of concrete steps. The riser nosing bar is bent 90° at each end. See Detail 57.

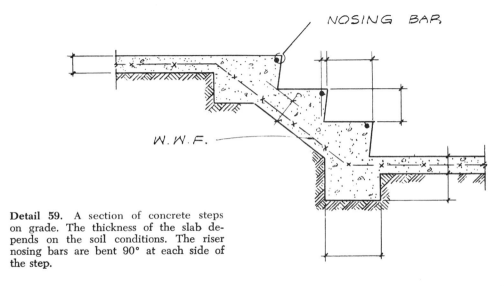

Detail 59. A section of concrete steps on grade. The thickness of the slab depends on the soil conditions. The riser nosing bars are bent 90° at each side of the step.

203

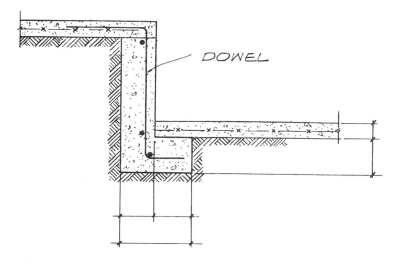

Detail 60. A section of a step of a concrete slab on grade. The thickness of the vertical wall of the step depends on the difference in elevations of the slabs on grade. The top slab is connected to the wall by reinforcing dowels.

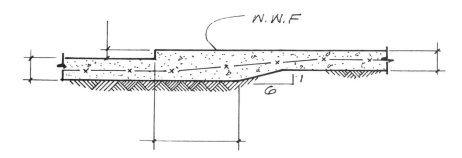

Detail 61. A section of a depressed concrete slab on grade. The slab is thickened at the edge of the depression for a length of 12".

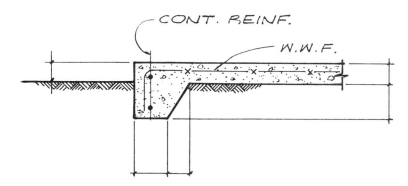

Detail 62. A section of the edge of a concrete slab on grade. The welded wire fabric is bent at the edge of the slab as shown. The reinforcing bars are nominal bars to prevent the slab from cracking.

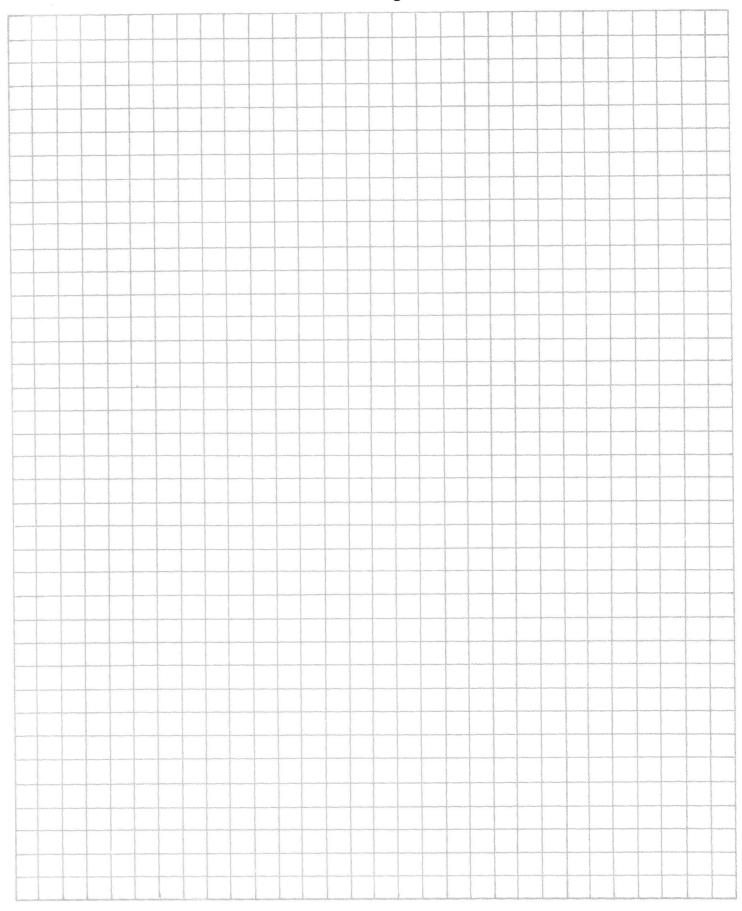

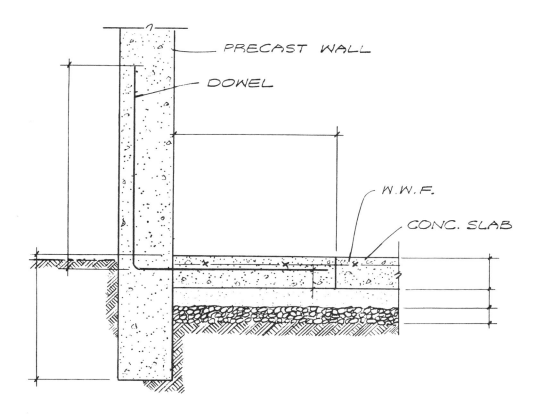

Detail 63(a). A section of the bottom of a precast concrete wall connected to a concrete slab on grade. The wall is connected to the slab by reinforcing dowels extending into the concrete slab and lapping with the slab welded wire fabric. The length of the dowel lap is determined by calculation. The perimeter of the slab is poured after the precast wall is erected in place.

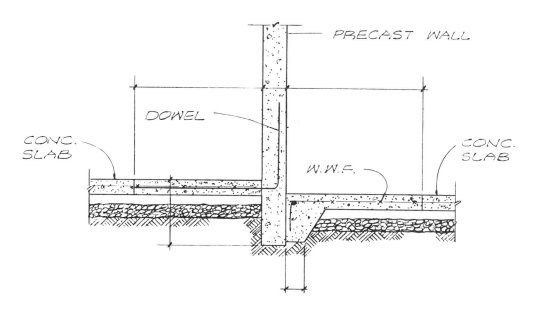

Detail 63(b). A section of a precast concrete wall connected to a concrete slab on grade similar to Detail 63(a).

207

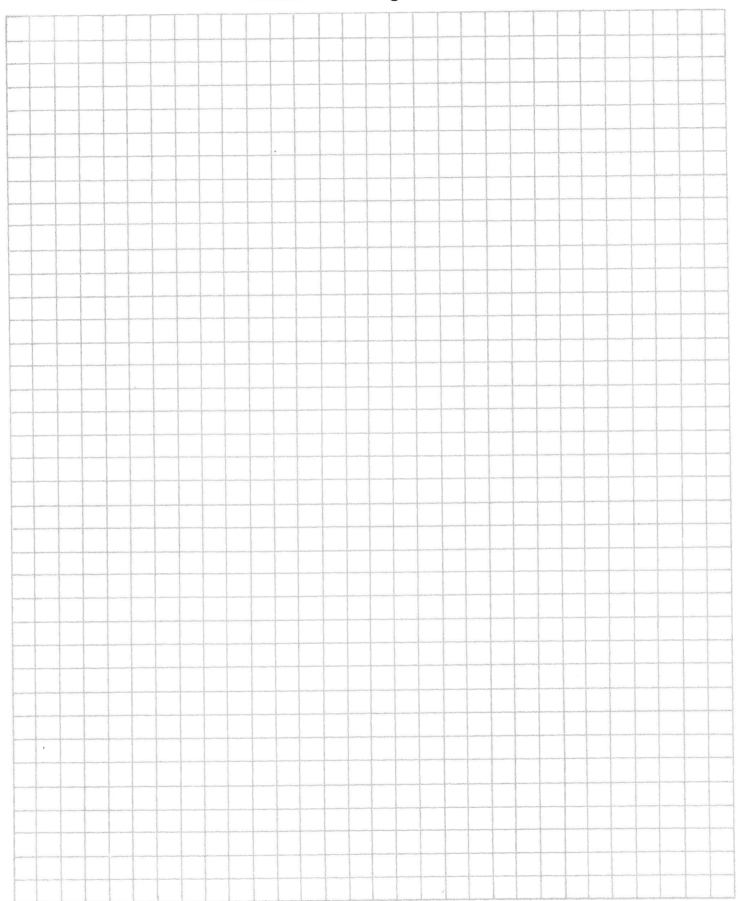

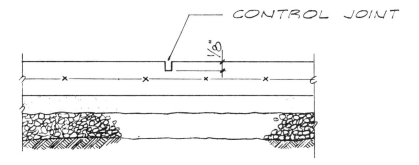

Detail 64(a). A section of a control joint in a concrete slab on grade. The depth and width of the joint are $^1/_8$" The purpose of this joint is to control the cracking of concrete slabs on grade.

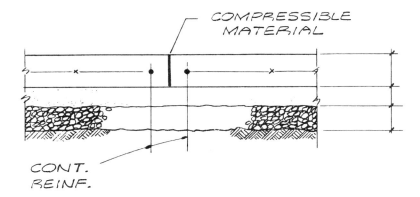

Detail 64(b). A section of a construction joint for a concrete slab on grade. The location of construction joints depends on the soil conditions and the use of the concrete slab.

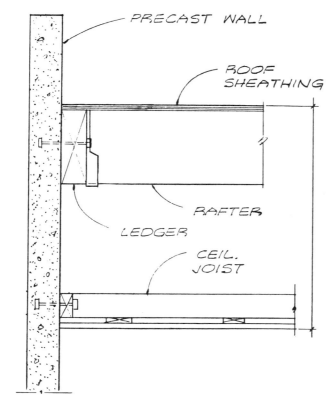

Detail 65. A section of a concrete wall, a wood roof and a wood ceiling. The roof rafters are connected to a 4″ wide wood ledger by joist hangers. The ledger is bolted to the concrete wall. The size and spacing of ledger bolts are determined by calculation. The ceiling joists are connected to a 2″ wide ledger bolted to the wall.

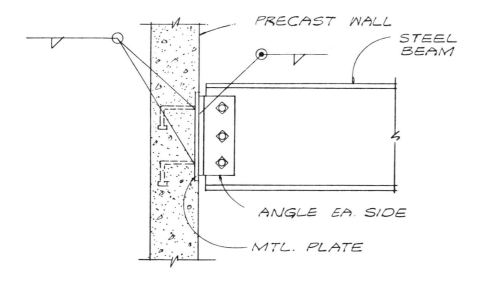

Detail 66. A section of a concrete wall and a steel beam. The clip angles are connected to the beam on each side of the web with bolts. The clip angles are connected to the wall by welding to a flat plate in the concrete wall.

211

Notes ▪ Drawings ▪ Ideas

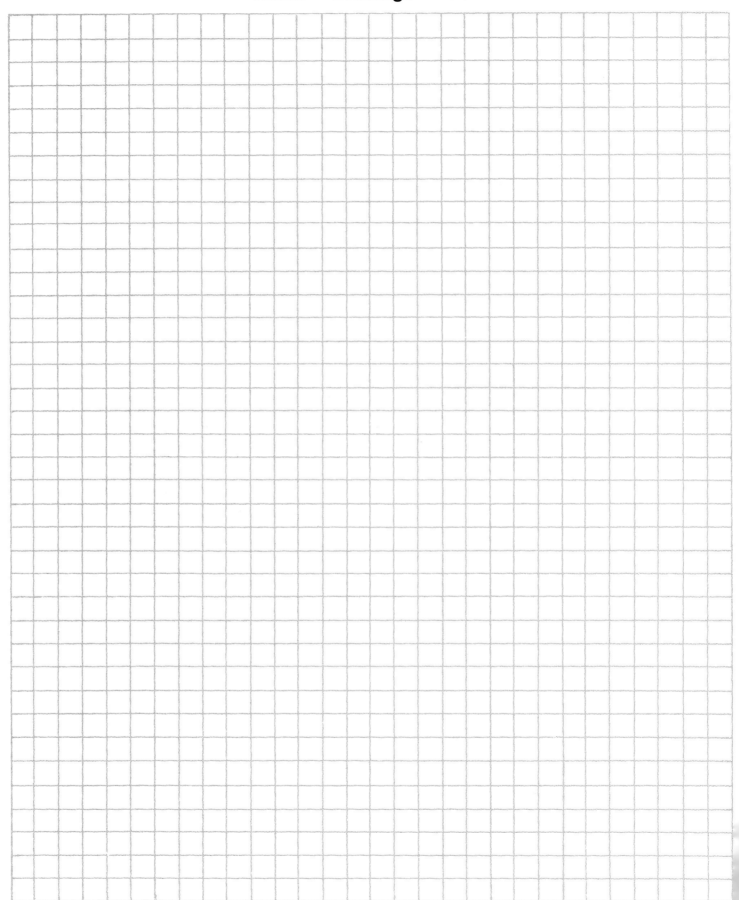

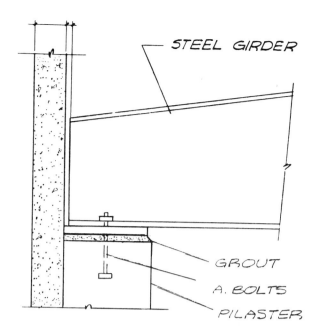

STEEL GIRDER

GROUT

A. BOLTS

PILASTER

Detail 67(a). An elevation of a tapered steel girder supported by a concrete pilaster. A space is provided between the end of the girder and the inside face of the concrete wall to allow for expansion and contraction of the girder. The girder is connected to the pilaster by a base plate set on a layer of grout. The anchor bolts pass through the bottom flange of the girder and the base plate. The bolt holes in the bottom flange of the girder are elongated to allow expansion and contraction movement. See Detail 67(b).

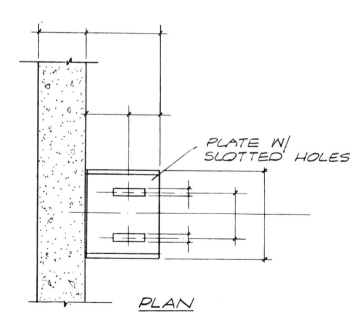

PLATE W/ SLOTTED HOLES

PLAN

Detail 67(b). A plan of the base plate used in Detail 67(a). The base plate holes are elongated as shown to permit the steel girder to move in expansion and contraction.

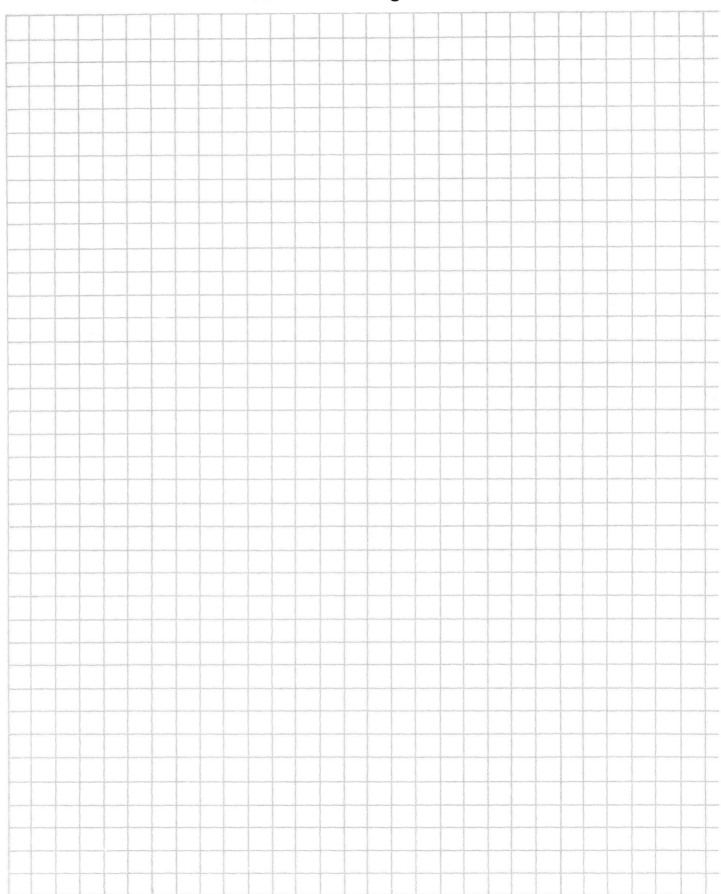

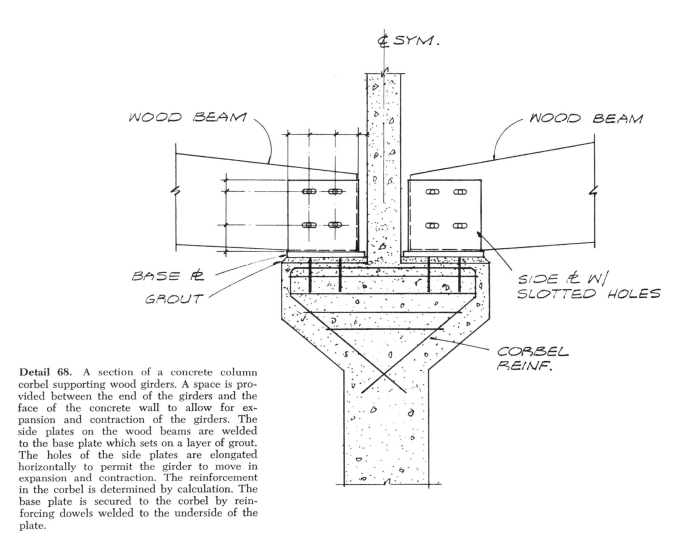

₵ SYM.

WOOD BEAM

WOOD BEAM

BASE ₱
GROUT

SIDE ₱ W/
SLOTTED HOLES

CORBEL
REINF.

Detail 68. A section of a concrete column corbel supporting wood girders. A space is provided between the end of the girders and the face of the concrete wall to allow for expansion and contraction of the girders. The side plates on the wood beams are welded to the base plate which sets on a layer of grout. The holes of the side plates are elongated horizontally to permit the girder to move in expansion and contraction. The reinforcement in the corbel is determined by calculation. The base plate is secured to the corbel by reinforcing dowels welded to the underside of the plate.

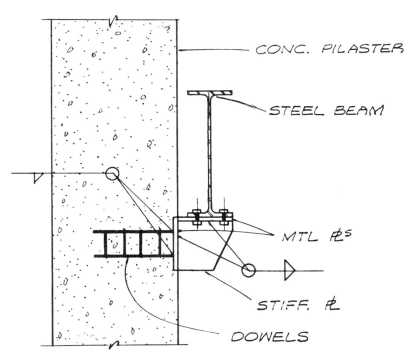

CONC. PILASTER

STEEL BEAM

MTL ₱ˢ

STIFF. ₱

DOWELS

Detail 69. A section of a concrete pilaster and a steel beam. The steel beam is supported by a metal bracket. The vertical stiffener of the bracket is welded to a flat plate in the concrete pilaster. The weld plate is connected to the pilaster with reinforcing dowels as shown. The pilaster reinforcement is not shown.

215

Notes ▪ Drawings ▪ Ideas

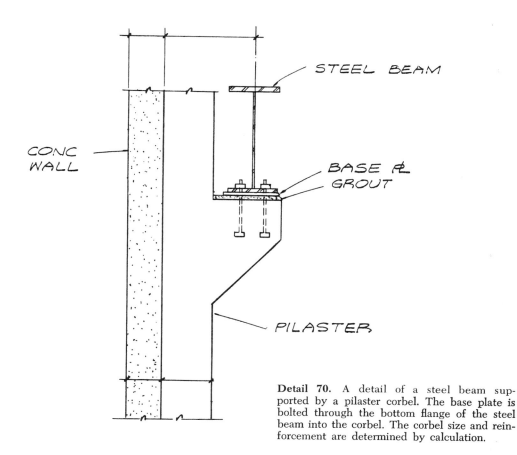

STEEL BEAM

CONC
WALL

BASE ℞
GROUT

PILASTER

Detail 70. A detail of a steel beam supported by a pilaster corbel. The base plate is bolted through the bottom flange of the steel beam into the corbel. The corbel size and reinforcement are determined by calculation.

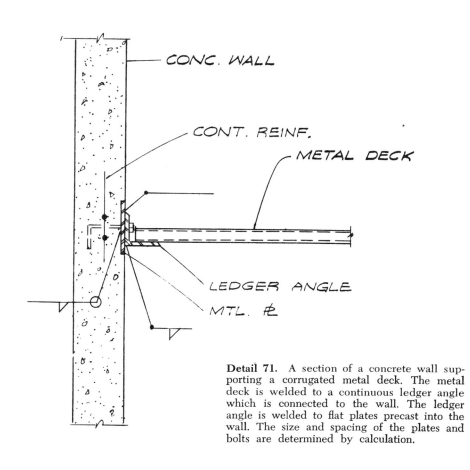

CONC. WALL

CONT. REINF.

METAL DECK

LEDGER ANGLE

MTL. ℞

Detail 71. A section of a concrete wall supporting a corrugated metal deck. The metal deck is welded to a continuous ledger angle which is connected to the wall. The ledger angle is welded to flat plates precast into the wall. The size and spacing of the plates and bolts are determined by calculation.

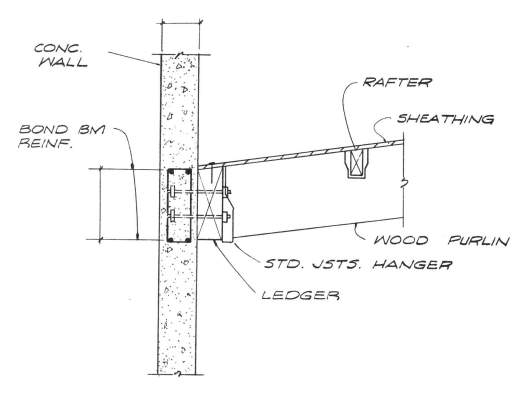

Detail 72. A section of a concrete wall supporting a wood ledger and purlin members of a panelized roof system. The purlins are connected to the ledger by standard joist hangers. The ledger is connected to the wall by bolts. The size and spacing of the ledger bolts are determined by calculation. The reinforcing bars in the wall act as a bond beam to resist the diaphragm shear stress.

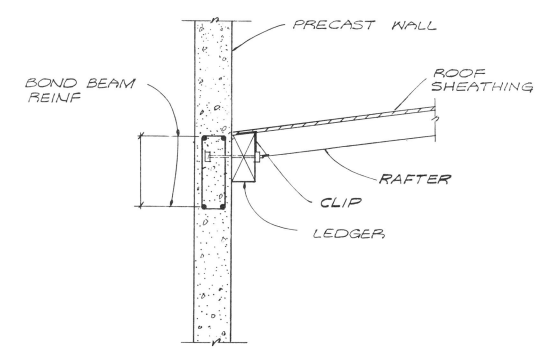

Detail 73. A section of a wall supporting the stiffner members of a panelized roof system. The 4″ wide ledger is bolted to the precast wall. The size and spacing of the ledger bolts are determined by calculation. The reinforcing bars in the wall act as a bond beam to resist the diaphragm shear stress.

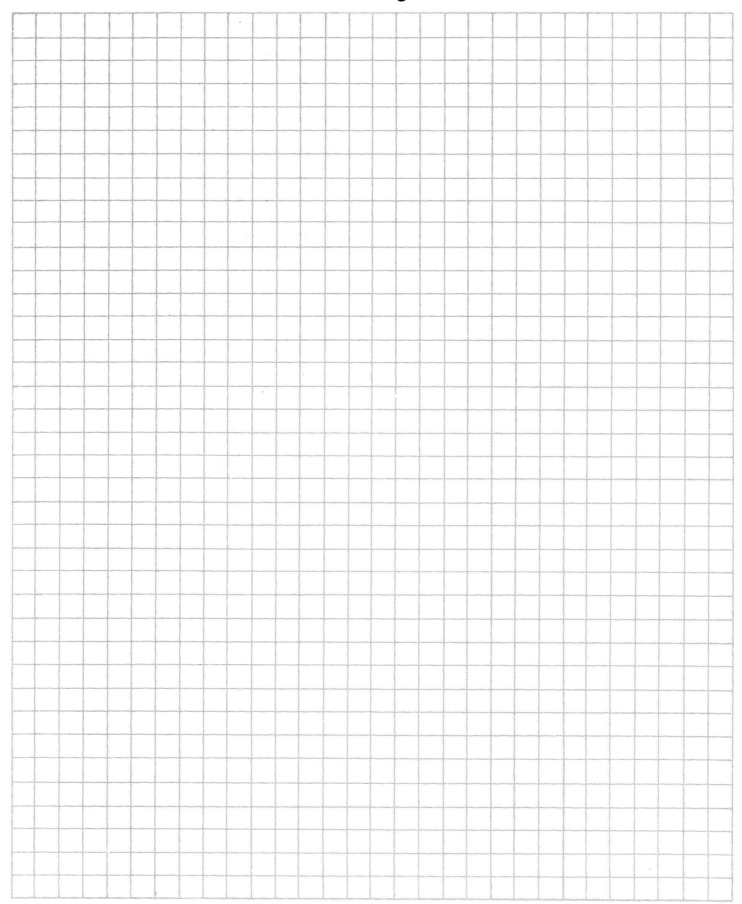

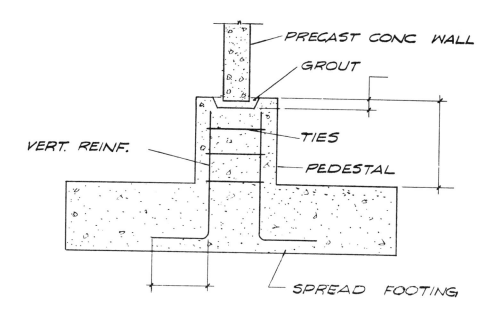

Detail 74(a). A section of a concrete spread footing and a precast concrete wall. The groove at the top of the pedestal is formed by a shaped 4″ wide wood member. The depth and width of the groove allow the precast wall to be placed and shimmed with metal plates to a level position. The groove is filled with grout after the precast wall is in place.

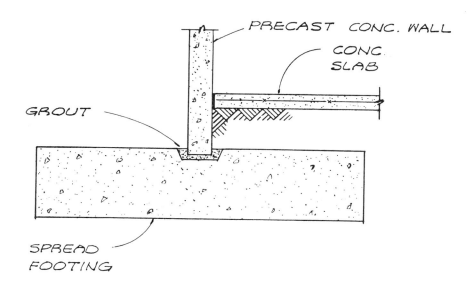

Detail 74(b). A section of a concrete spread footing and a precast concrete wall. The groove at the top of the footing is formed by a 4″ wide wood member. The depth and width of the groove allow the precast wall to be placed and shimmed with metal plates to a level position. The groove is filled with grout after the precast wall is in place.

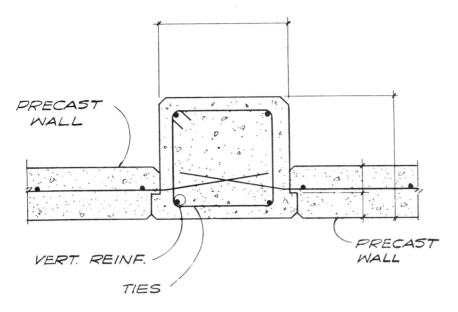

PRECAST WALL

VERT. REINF.

TIES

PRECAST WALL

Detail 75(a). A plan section of precast concrete walls connected to a poured concrete column. The walls are connected to the column by extending the wall horizontal reinforcing steel into the poured column 20 bar diameters.

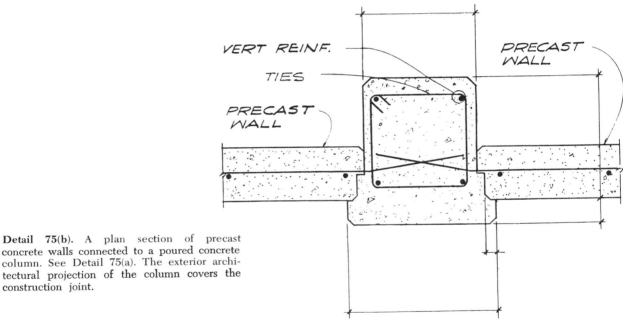

VERT REINF.

TIES

PRECAST WALL

PRECAST WALL

Detail 75(b). A plan section of precast concrete walls connected to a poured concrete column. See Detail 75(a). The exterior architectural projection of the column covers the construction joint.

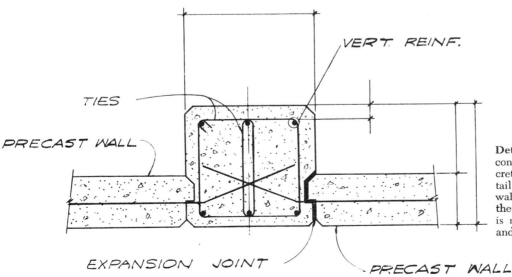

VERT. REINF.

TIES

PRECAST WALL

EXPANSION JOINT

PRECAST WALL

Detail 75(c). A plan section of precast concrete walls connected to a poured concrete column. This detail is similar to Detail 75(a). A joint between the precast wall and the column is made to permit the wall to expand and contract. The joint is made of a compressible solid material and coated with a waterproofing material.

Notes • Drawings • Ideas

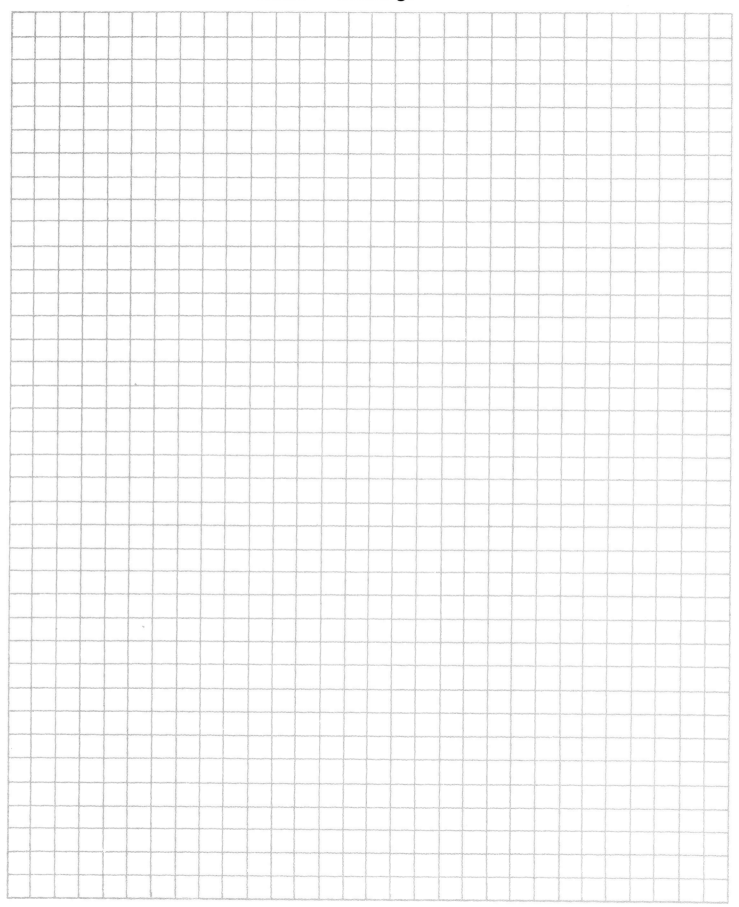

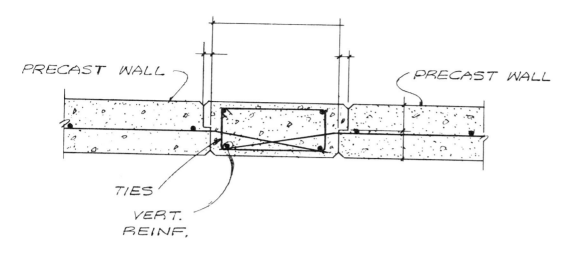

Detail 76(a). A plan section of precast concrete walls joined by a poured concrete splice connection. The horizontal bars of the precast wall are lapped 20 bar diameters in the poured splice. The poured splice is reinforced with four vertical bars as shown.

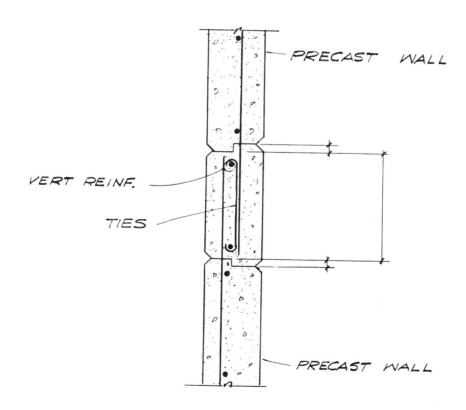

Detail 76(b). A plan section of precast concrete walls joined by a poured concrete splice connection. The horizontal bars of the precast wall are lapped 20 bar diameters in the poured splice. The poured splice is reinforced with two vertical bars as shown.

225

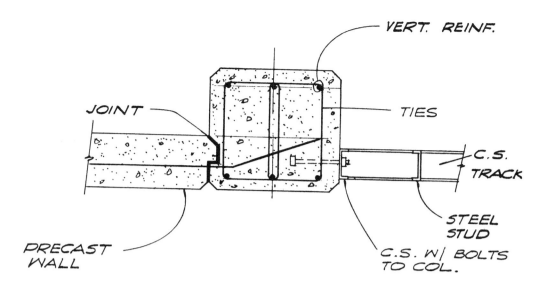

Detail 77. A plan section of a precast concrete wall and steel stud wall connected to a poured concrete column. The precast wall is connected to the poured concrete column as shown in Detail 75(c). The steel stud wall is connected to the poured column by bolting a channel track stud to the face of the column.

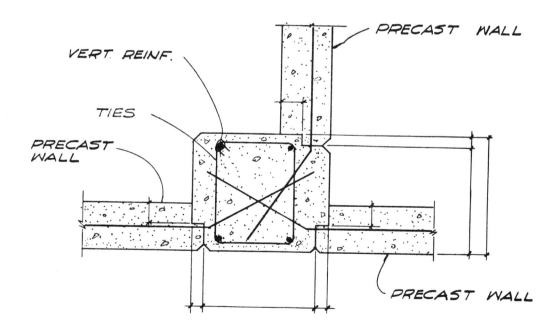

Detail 78. A plan section of precast concrete walls at a corner poured concrete column. The horizontal reinforcing bars of the walls are bent and lapped in the poured concrete column as shown.

Notes · Drawings · Ideas

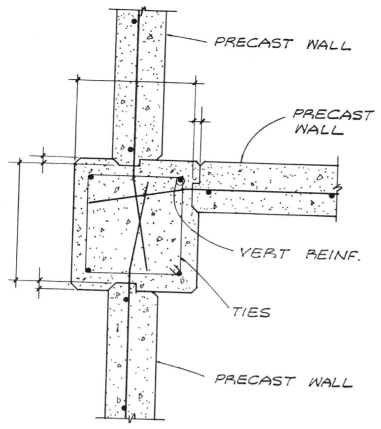

Detail 79. A plan section of precast concrete walls and a poured corner splice joint. The horizontal reinforcing bars of the precast walls are extended 20 bar diameters into the poured corner splice.

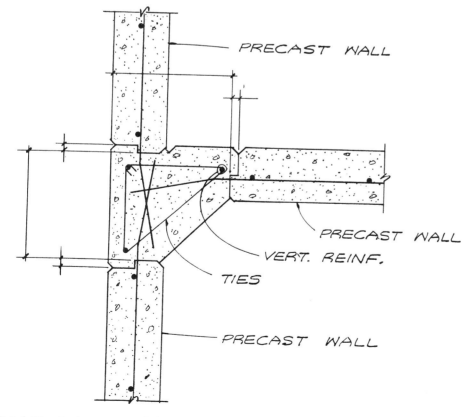

Detail 80. A plan section of three precast concrete walls intersecting at a poured concrete column. The horizontal reinforcing bars of the wall extend 20 bar diameters into the poured column.

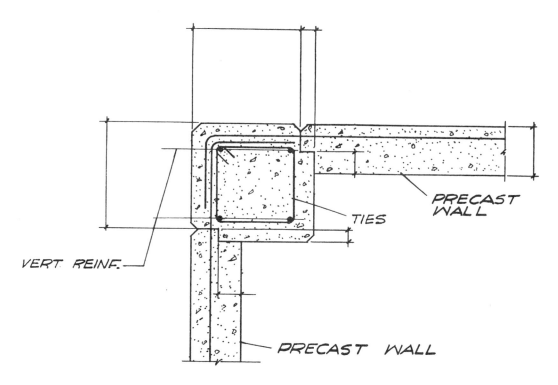

Detail 81. A plan section of three precast concrete walls intersecting at a poured concrete column. See Detail 80.

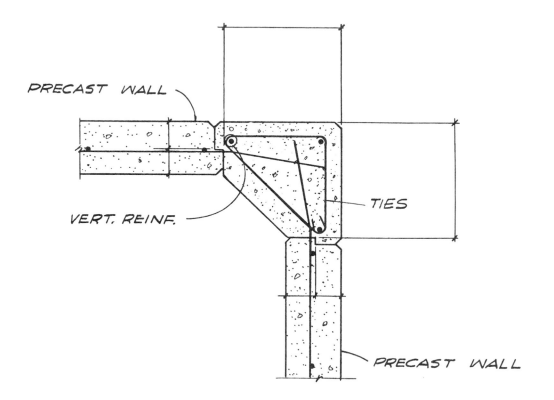

Detail 82. A plan section of three precast concrete walls intersecting at a poured concrete splice. See Detail 80.

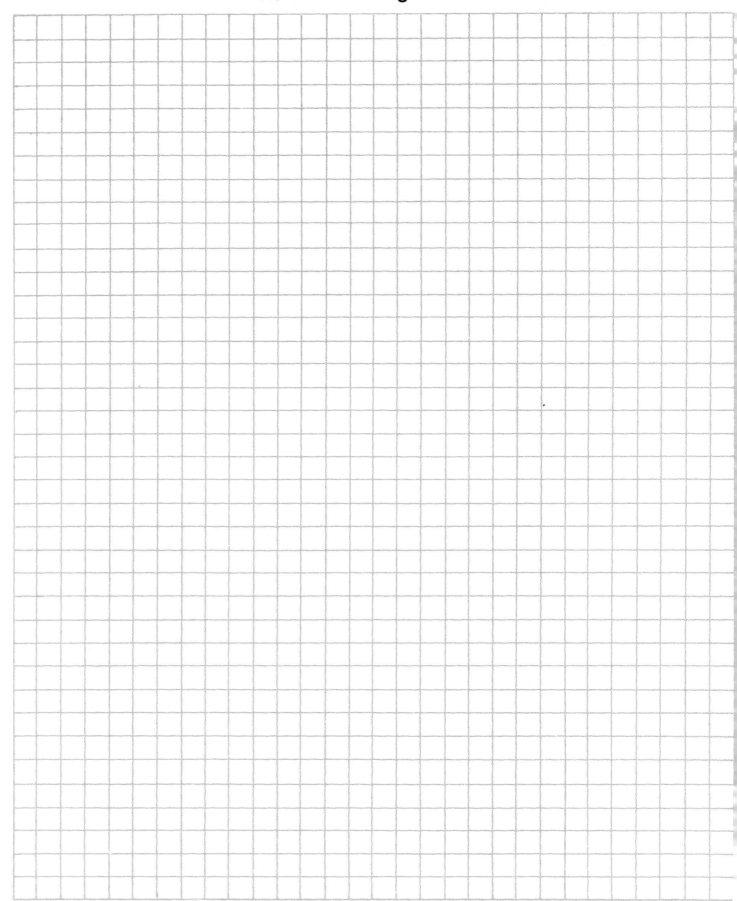

INDEX